EBURY PRESS

THE SHOONYAM QUOTIENT

Dr Mickey Mehta, a global leader in holistic health and a corporate spiritual coach, boasts an impressive fifty-three years of yoga experience and has been professionally active for forty-four years.

He was recently appointed by HDFC ERGO's Habit of Life campaign as the 'Face of the Movement' in association with the Best Places to Work initiative.

In addition, he was awarded the title of 'Leading Icon of Holistic Wellness' by the *Economic Times* in 2018. He has also received prestigious accolades such as the 'Health and Wellness Icon of India' from the *Economic Times* and was honoured with the Jagran Award on 14 June 2024 under the 'Special Recognition' category of Pioneer of Holistic Health in India for his forty-four years of service in the health industry.

Dr Mehta was also appointed as professor of practice for holistic health at HSNC University, Mumbai. He was also honoured by the Indian Association of Switzerland during the seventy-fifth anniversary of Azadi ka Amrit Mahotsav for being a pioneer in holistic health in India.

He has authored four books: *The Shoonyam Quotient, Lose Weight Gain Shape, Immunity+* with super chef Sanjeev Kapoor, and *Weightless: Unburden*. His upcoming books include *Focus to Lotus, Curd Karma* and *Woman: The Healer*.

He has also published several medical research papers in renowned journals. He has also been a speaker at Harvard University, IIMs and IITs.

Appointed as a FIT India Movement Champion by the Sports Authority of India, Dr Mehta has achieved a significant milestone in promoting fitness and wellness. He was also the first-ever columnist, as well as a television and radio presenter, focusing on wellness.

He has served as a life coach to billionaires in India Inc., Bollywood superstars, top politicians, multiple Miss Worlds and Miss Universes, members of the police force, the Indian army and others.

The Shoonyam Quotient

The Light of Life

• —— •

DR MICKEY MEHTA

Global Leading Holistic Health Guru

EBURY
PRESS

An imprint of Penguin Random House

EBURY PRESS

Ebury Press is an imprint of the Penguin Random House group of companies
whose addresses can be found at global.penguinrandomhouse.com

Published by Penguin Random House India Pvt. Ltd
4th Floor, Capital Tower 1, MG Road,
Gurugram 122 002, Haryana, India

First published in Ebury Press by Penguin Random House India 2017
This edition published in 2024

10 9 8 7

ISBN 9780143441342

Typeset in Sabon by Manipal Digital Systems, Manipal
Printed at Replika Press Pvt. Ltd, India

www.penguin.co.in

I dedicate my book to:

Lao Tzu
Maharishi Mahesh Yogi
B.K.S. Iyengar
Osho Rajneesh
Baba Ramdev
Sri Sri Ravi Shankar
Sadhguru Jaggi Vasudev
Shri Avdhoot Baba Shivanand
and, above all, Deepak Chopra

This book would not have been possible without the
monumental help of my friend Kshitij Negi.

Contents

Preface

I am not the author; I am just a medium. People before me have spoken a lot and people after me will also say a lot—all I have done is added my perspective, personal experience and learning with wisdom collected through the prism of my mind and the eyes of my soul to what others have already said.

Life reveals its secrets from time to time via circumstances, situations and events. Where I am today, someone else was yesterday and somebody else will be tomorrow. I am sure after you read this you will get optimized and get Mickeymized!

Humanity = Divinity

1

COGNITIVE OVERLOAD? PLEASE OFFLOAD

Cognitive overload is as heavy as it sounds. It can significantly impact motivation, energy levels and overall mental well-being. The overload is a consequence of multitasking and overstimulation. To combat such mental clutter, one can adhere to a structured dietary regimen known as 'Information Fasting', which involves reducing the overwhelming influx of information bombarding you from every direction.

Prioritize your tasks, practise mindlessness, participate in physical activities, dedicate time to relax, practise deep breathing exercises, break down complex tasks into manageable steps, and seek support from friends, family or even professionals.

The concept of intermittent fasting can be introduced for better physical and mental health. For instance, eating only during an eight-hour daily window and fasting for the remaining sixteen hours

(16/8). The same principle can be applied here: stop consuming through your senses or through your lenses.

SELF-HEALING, SELF-TALK IN UNISON WITH THE UNIVERSE

Food is to your body what thoughts are to your mind. Both serve as fuel and affect our well-being. While initiating *internal dialogue* can create and sustain motivation, optimistic self-talk acts as a nourisher for the mind. Creating various beautiful aspects of life, even amidst challenging situations, can help retain your equilibrium and inspire you to do your best.

An optimistic mental being is crucial. You need to ask yourself how you want to feel. Come up with new mantras until you strike self-talk gold.

Talking in the present tense, conversing with 'Be' and incorporating effective emotions are effective methods of self-talk. Each opportunity is a blessing, hence actively pursue every dream and desire, and connect with the universal source every day. Be happy and calm, foster intuition, and engage in creative actions daily to make quantum leaps of progress while embracing limitless.

Condition yourself with the attitude that 'I am here to impact.' I am here to 'Be' and 'Evolve'. Embrace and internalize what nature has to offer, without looking away.

SLIP INTO YOUR OWN SANCTUARY

Be in a quiet space, where you can escape the cacophony of the outside world. Retreat to this space to gather yourself, unwind and engage in deep breathing exercises. Life in the centre is a life of celebration as opposed to life on the circumference, which is a life of suffering.

FIND YOUR DEEP-DIVE DIVINITY

Find your divinity in absolute silence and self-reflection. In these tranquil moments, watch your thoughts, feelings, desires and emotions. The source of sacredness lies deep within each human being. As we levitate, we find the higher state, which is much above our intellect, where we can hear the unheard and see the unseen. This is what we call our true self, our spontaneous existence, or even our soul—Aatma.

The Upanishads say: 'Man is not man, Man is God.' But to encounter this amazing reality, it takes a lot of work. Our body is a temple and our soul is God.

When your true inner self is awakened, magic happens.

BE THE MASTER OF CREATIVITY

Creativity is inherent to human consciousness. Only a human being can rise above God and descend below animals. Creativity extends beyond the material world to encompass the complexities of each of our unique existences.

Every individual is a highly intricate work of art, a masterpiece and a manifestation of the universal energies. Our creative expressions can be an outcome of *Sankalp* and *Siddhi* (determination and attainment), in the form of worship, meditation, enhancement of the self and wholeness of the soul.

All creativity starts in a state of blissful ignorance, with graceful submission, acceptance and willingness to be vulnerable. We can let the divine and creative energy flow through us and manifest like a bewildered child who is in wonderment of his being, with pure emotions flowing out into the world. As an epicentre of this expression, we become an embodiment of this being.

Humans normally breathe about twenty-two times in a minute. When it slows down to fifteen breaths per minute, we begin to understand deeper languages, perceive more colours, and gain clearer perceptions and perspectives. Breathing below fifteen times per minute enables us to understand the language of the elements of nature—the sky, the ocean, air. When breathing fewer than ten breaths per minute, we begin to comprehend the language of birds and bees. And with fewer than five breaths a minute, we understand all languages of the universe.

You have now arrived at a state of metacognition—this term literally means 'above cognition'. It is an awareness of one's thought processes and an understanding of the patterns behind them.

In a state of metacognition, you start reflecting on your ways of thinking and knowing when and how to use strategies for problem-solving.

Optimism is the new theism. When your mind is full, it is cluttered; when empty, it is illuminated with awareness. In a state of mindlessness and emptiness, spontaneity and divinity emerge.

So, empty your mind and mind the emptiness.

Paranoid Humanoid

2

The very fact that you are holding this book is proof that you consider yourself to be a human being. Yet, this book is not here to reinforce that belief. In fact, this book will challenge all those beliefs. I must warn you that it can get painful if you are not prepared to confront some extreme beliefs we all hold.

If you refuse to look at yourself, rediscover yourself and finally be your true, wonderful, complete self, then this is not the book for you.

Human being. Being human. What is it really to be human?

Not so very long ago, the planet was inhabited by a species called Homo sapiens. In a number of ways, it was a weak species. It did not have the raw physical strength to overpower other species for food, nor did it have sharp claws or teeth to compensate for its lack of muscular strength. It didn't have any poisonous glands to make its prey unconscious.

So how did the species survive? It had something that more than made up for all of these handicaps.

It had a jelly-like floating mass in its skull called the brain. This brain had intelligence that was far superior to all other species. Homo sapiens made good use of this intelligence to stay warm in the winters, sheltered during the long rains and safe against ferocious animals.

It all began with the instinct to survive. But then emerged the instinct for art and the wonder for nature. Homo sapiens began to paint on the walls of their caves.

They found a way to grow food and rear livestock, eliminating the need to hunt for food. They stayed in groups and evolved communication techniques, which turned into languages. And their thirst for knowledge only grew. Culture, science, entertainment, spirituality and other aspects of the human quest took shape. The evolution of the Homo sapiens to 'human' was nearing completion and the stage was set for the next level. But . . .

Intelligence developed and thought processes grew from simple to complex, complex to complicated and from complicated to downright chaotic. Fear wouldn't let any of these experiences be lived completely, and greed would not let any of these be let go of, for there was so much more to be experienced. Almost as an eddy in the great scheme of evolution, as if against the natural order of things, another species evolved. I call it the Paranoid Humanoid.

The extent of changes that took place over thousands of years was surpassed by the changes in the last few centuries; and the changes in the last few centuries were exceeded by what ensued in the last few decades. Till just a few years ago, we were still working on what to do with our time—inventing and perfecting arts, crafts, knowledge and rituals in the process. And now, everyone only seems to complain of not ever having time.

Compare the years of Homo sapiens on earth to the years of civilized existence. Given the way the next wave of 'no time' and infinite information and things have become all pervasive, it almost feels as if that in-between phase of evolution never existed.

Look at the life of a Paranoid Humanoid (PH). Her day begins with an alarm going off. What a way to begin your day—being ALARMED. Sleep hasn't gently given way to movement. She gets up because she *has* to, with a start. And among the 2000-odd reasons why she didn't sleep as much as she really wanted, these are just a few—she *had* to attend that social do, she *had* to complete that report, she *had* to watch that movie and she *had* to help her daughter complete her science project.

He gets up with a bad hangover and picks up his newspaper, a daily source of negativity—with its front page full of the latest on deaths, devastations, corruption and scandals. He lights his cigarette to ensure bowel movement. There is scarcely time for a quick shower and the gobbling down of breakfast.

Could the PH be seeking to obviate the negativity by filling his dissatisfied being with more and more?

There is nothing wrong with having more—more varieties of food, more clothes of the latest fashion, more choices in books, films, television programmes and travel destinations. Yet, the dissipation of energy through greed brings about a life of consumption. Before you have savoured your appetizer completely, you fill your mouth with your drink. Before your senses enjoy the feel of a new dress on your body, you throw it away, lest someone finds you wearing the same outfit twice. Before the message has seeped in, you have already turned the page, tossed the book aside, or changed the channel. The funny thing is that after experiencing all this you are astonished as to why you are not feeling fulfilled. The astonishing thing is that you are astonished by this!

Whether you are an executive or unemployed, a stay-at-home person, a senior citizen or a youngster, this is the DNA of your life.

While eating a sandwich, you have important conversations to complete, reminders to be set and mails to be sent out. If it's not any of these, you have to think about the next call to be made, what direction your conversation could take and what your counter-arguments could be. Did you also brood over what your boss said yesterday and the heartache caused by your secret rival's latest success?

Now imagine, if eating a simple sandwich involves so much work, how much of those seven minutes is spent purely eating the sandwich? That's the PH existence. Incomplete. Broken. Partial. Disintegrated. Unfulfilled.

At some level, the PH also recognizes this but thinks that there is only one tool that can compensate for it or fix it—MORE. We are filled with paranoia every time we have felt this anxiety and sense of incompleteness. Paranoia feeds on its own fuel and perpetuates it. We work harder, we work longer and we try to earn more money, recognition, degrees, and what have you.

Have you ever seen any car being stopped by stepping on the gas? And yet, haven't you seen panicky drivers pressing the accelerator instead of the brake? Don't you press the accelerator of paranoia when you want to manage the car of your life?

Yes, it is a moment of bewilderment. I can see the PH looking at me with his mouth open. Bewildered, because he has never known any other way to exist. When you have less, you put in more. When you get fewer marks in one exam, you put in more hours of study for the next. When you have less sweetness in your life, you add more sugar in your coffee. The one formula we have come to live by is MORE, MORE, MORE.

So much so that we have ceased to look at what it is that we are putting in more of! Are you putting in more sugar to make the coffee sweeter or to make yourself happy?

If there is distortion in the lenses of your glasses, do you add more distorted lenses to fix your sight?

When the child of a PH is not performing at school, he gets anxious. Almost every time the grades of even a monthly test are declared, the PH begins thinking of what it is that needs to be done to increase the child's marks. If the grades are low in mathematics, she has to devote more hours to the subject. Or more money should be spent on a better (read, costlier) tutor or books.

And if that still that does not work, the child should do more of something else. More art classes, more sports . . . Just more. The child should somehow feed the PH's desire for more.

When the spouse of a PH is not healing, the PH gets more and more doctors, who prescribe more and more medicines. She doesn't know any better.

Putting more and more colour on a canvas does not a make a painting any better.

Whether one is human or a Humanoid is the dilemma of modern life. And even this dilemma remains hidden for, or denied by, most. Where is the urban educated standing today? There is so much disintegration in her life. The irony is that the PH is able to see all these pitfalls and, yet, refuses to acknowledge their existence or hides behind the order of the world. She denies her own role in anything.

Every Humanoid stands dispersed. So many times we hear others around us or find ourselves saying, 'I have to get the pieces of my life together. Life is much too scattered. Let me consolidate myself.' Yet, rarely do we go beyond the basic quick fixes.

As a species, we have the arrogance to think that our structures, created in a few hundred years, will take the place of what Nature has evolved in a million years. The suicidal pace at which we are destroying Nature's creations is becoming irreversible. There are fallouts all around us, but we don't even want to acknowledge the collapse of life—life, as it should be. The results are for everyone to see. Every crisis is solved with a grander solution needing evermore complicated systems. We are being enslaved by one thing after another, each one of our own creation.

An important aspect of our existence is the deep bond we share with the people in our lives and also with all of existence in all its varied manifestations. But this deep bonding has given way to trappings and bondages.

The whole idea of bonding begins when the baby is conceived. But it comes alive during labour. The imminent separation bothers both the mother and the child inside the womb. The pain of letting go makes that bond come alive.

As soon as the child emerges from the womb, the baby feels a sense of huge insecurity. Insecurity caused by emerging from the warm environs it has known for nine months into the unknown. Not just that, but the disconnection with the umbilical cord leaves the baby totally disoriented. She wonders, 'Where am I?' And that is the cry that bursts out of the child. If you look at it physiologically, that cry is good. It exercises the lungs and makes the child breathe. Because of the outburst of sound, the air gets released and breathing begins. A child doesn't breathe first; she displaces air first. The child goes on displacing air from then on and keeps making space naturally for herself as she grows. But the manner in which childhood is supported decides what she will really bloom into.

We express dismay that children have no regard for their elders any more. But why does that happen? It happens because the touch and bond that keeps respect alive is already missing in the life of the little

Humanoid. At the worst, a PH mother is too eager to give up breastfeeding, to go back to work or to partying. And a PH father holds back his emotions, trapped in the cage of masculinity. Such PH parents often prefer to spend time earning money to buy more things. There isn't enough time to love the child or there is not enough love to spend time with the child. There is no substitute for a loving, nurturing home environment. The PH thinks that this can come from material comforts, bigger homes, better jobs, luxury cars, innumerable toys and clothes. And yet, it doesn't make anyone happy.

A lot of stress is laid on encouraging children to have separate identities and be independent from their parents. An oft-debated topic among urban families is whether children should sleep with their parents. Children, especially infants, should be welcomed to sleep with their parents. Otherwise, the child is fed with signals, one after the other, that he is unwanted. And this grows into an unshakeable belief in him, deep down in the subconscious. Parents are turning their children into PHs from birth. The seed of being Humanoid is further nurtured in the child as he observes his parents. And yet, we are surprised at how they turn out.

Mothers are the first to be blamed if the child turns out to be problematic. This is because they are the primary caretakers. The first contact a new life has with another human being. It is most critical for parents to start looking at what they are really providing for their children. Not in terms of material comforts, but with regard to their long-term psychological health. Both parents need to address some difficult and rather grim questions about the environment they create for their children. How do they become distorted and grow into Humanoids? The answer lies in the fact that as we become Humanoids instead of humans, so do our children.

Look around and notice your surroundings. Check the direction in which progress is marching. Realize that a time will come when we will become completely mechanical. Modern man has stagnated or is regressing to become procedural and mechanical. Instead of being intelligent, the species is trapped in the cause and effect. If we continue as is, there will be no intelligence, no creativity and no sensuality left in us. That is what is happening to us.

PHs are living as if this is the last generation. How ironical that though at the existential level he is farthest from the here and now, at another level, he behaves as if he will always remain this age, will never grow old and his children will never grow older. And so he goes on to create dubious gifts for future generations.

The effects of this irresponsible behaviour are beyond the domain of a personal or collective will of a single generation. This generation, in fact, stands more as a symbol of degeneration, which seems to be manifesting as psychological disorders, passing on through the DNA to the next generation. This is seen in the alarming trend of a disconcerting rise in the number of children suffering from juvenile diabetes and asthma, and so many other disorders.

Stop for a minute and visualize the significant ways in which one shows one's affection to children—playing with them, hugging them, talking to them and telling stories. Now imagine the victims of a PH—children whose parents don't have time to hug and hold them, leave alone play with them. They are often left with the house help, who attend to their basic needs. But what about emotional and intellectual needs?

When we can't live properly, we can't die properly. Too many human beings today are dying of diseases. Is that the only way to die now? Surely not! Why should they not pass away peacefully?

We plant seeds that give us fruit in some years. A tree takes a certain amount of time to bloom and prosper. The tree has no economic logic of its own— when it should yield fruits for maximum profit. Someone has to plant trees without being bothered about when the fruits are going to ripen and who is going to consume them. Once you are attached to the outcome of your doing, you are anxious and fearful about it, or ambitious, lustful and greedy about it. In these conditions, you are bound to make mistakes, bound to meet disasters. And you are not total in the act.

You cannot avoid the system, nor am I advising you to do so; I am merely telling you *how* you can go through it without getting affected by it. Your here–now is and is *the* only potential field for the manifestation of your true self. So if you are not total in that, you have missed out on a lot. And how can you not be total? If you are thinking or reflecting upon the past or projecting, planning and scheming about the future, then you are missing out on your HERE–NOW completely.

The absence of being whole, being total, leads to the degeneration, disintegration and erosion of the being. It further feeds on itself and takes you down a negative spiral. From being human beings, we become Humanoids—scheming, plotting and strategizing. We are so busy doing things that are constantly taking us from one level of being unfulfilled to another that there is no time to enjoy the moments in life that actually bring fulfilment. Purity of action in spontaneity and faith is singularly missing in the existence of Humanoids.

Human beings are subject to time, matter, space, light, motion, mass, causation, effect and gravity, and get influenced by them. But not the way Humanoids do. Humanoids are on a rampage to get rid of time, motion and space by creating complicated machines and chemicals. They are fighting light, matter and mass. They hone a vengeance against a reflection of themselves, a projection of themselves, the very essence of themselves. And they think they can win in this battle. And what can you win when there is no battle to fight? You need to drop your guard and give up on the idea of this illusory fight against nature. If you are perpetually in the realization of being one with nature, what is the point of fighting and what is there to win?

All the pleasures and indulgences make you live a life that is at a very low level. You are just living from surface to surface. You have forgotten that there was never a beginning, never a middle and never an end. You are running in circles, forgetting that a circle is a big zero—a *shoonya*. And yet, in that shoonya lies the ultimate peace, your Shoonyam Quotient.

Get maximized, get Mickeymized!

Chase Maze

3

Don't run away from life. But don't keep running in life. Running is what you do in a chase. We are running all the time in our lives; running in a maze. We delude ourselves into thinking there is an end to this maze, just around the corner. There, at the end of the rainbow, lies all that will compensate for this running and this chasing of dreams we indulge in.

But here is the bad news: there is no such place round the corner in the Chase Maze. There is only an endless, perpetually winding labyrinthine maze.

There's no stopping in this Chase Maze. One is only likely to collapse, exhausted, one day. Funnily, in all likelihood, a PH won't even notice the signs of fatigue or saturation till—well, what else but—he actually collapses. And the doctor diagnoses a slipped disc, an ulcer, a stroke or a heart condition. And then the situation unfolds. The PH's first reaction is a lament: 'Why me?' But these words were not uttered when there was a chance to take a cruise during that last vacation. Or when he upgraded his car.

Almost immediately follows the vehement claim—'it happened all of a sudden!' Yeah, right! Who had that heartburn for the last two years? Haven't headaches and constant fatigue been your loyal companions? They were the benevolent messengers who gently kept tapping to remind you of what was coming, and you royally ignored them in your blind arrogance.

Even life-threatening health conditions are nothing but more assertive messengers forcing you to look at your own lifestyle. Indulgence, denial, blame and finally . . . acceptance! Do you have to keep going through this cycle? Or is there a better path to follow?

Every Paranoid Humanoid is running. And running so fast that she cannot even see what she is running towards. Time and again, she feels a bump and she feels she has passed this rough road before, but she refuses to stop. She cannot afford to step back and assess what it is she is really running for or towards or away from. Nor has she the time to stop and notice that the ladder she is climbing up so fast is perhaps leaning against the wrong wall. She has no time to look at what she is chasing and what she is missing! She has no clue that it is a maze she is running in and she has no clue where she will be at the end of the chase.

Why is it a maze? It is a maze because a person literally gets caught inside it. And why is it a chase? Because desires being chased always remain alluringly ahead. Also, a person gets caught up in the whirlpool of experiences. And it is a Chase Maze because by being caught up in collecting experiences, one perpetuates the cycle of karma.

Karma is nothing but pure action. An action is neither good nor bad, if you look at it in the parlance of the universal, holistic view. Devoid of completion, devoid of totality, all that one keeps doing is collecting. One collects it because one is not doing anything with totality, so one cannot transcend it.

Let's say you are eating food. This means you are in the midst of an experience, the experience of eating food. You are experiencing the aroma, the taste and the touch, in addition to the subtle sense of security and satiation. But the satiation and awareness of having your food is not total because at the same time, you are thinking about what could be happening at work, that your wife has to be picked up from some place or about your child's higher education. Now, since the experience of eating remains unfulfilled, you are not total. You may feel full and feel saturated, but deep down, you are not satiated. Only when you are truly satiated is when freedom from experience is gained. Then there is no memory significant enough to create an action towards it.

Now think about how you spend time with your child. You are playing a game, say with building blocks. Your child is watching and getting involved with the process. And then your phone buzzes. It's a text message and you feel the urgent need to check it right there and then. Not only that, you also proceed to reply. Your child is watching, waiting. You turn your back to him, and it pings again. And again you reply. Are you spending time with your child or your phone? And then your child pulls and tugs at you for your attention. You get annoyed and push him away. What are you creating? An attention-hungry individual. You are there with him but not really there. You are creating an unloved, dissatisfied individual. No satiation here for parental affection.

Look at the cycle of karma again. You collect an experience and that experience becomes a memory. Memory creates a desire for more such experiences (or a desire to avoid an unpleasant experience). But if you are total, completely satiated, then the desire is completely dissolved.

When there is no desire, there is no significant build-up of memory in a way that will haunt you. It will not become an obsession because nothing has been repressed there.

Like when you are having sex, you are thinking of many other things, so you are never fulfilled by sex; therefore, you become obsessed with it. Sex may make you forget everything for some moments but that is not the same as being completely in it. What you get at times is only a glimpse of the completion and the transcendence that is possible, not the completion itself. And so it is with food. And so too for everything in your life. Only when this cycle is broken are you free from the consequences.

Human beings, even at the time of birth, are not at any definite point. A definite point is achieved only when they are centred. This is a point in infinity. But before centring, they live in a finite world. They go through life, collecting experiences and even at the time of death are not centred.

Neither birth nor death is a definite point because the wheel is constantly turning. It has begun at an arbitrary point and will end at an arbitrary point. It is only when one goes through that one can be centred. But it is not a definite location. It is not in space either because it is space-less and time-less.

You cannot do anything with desires just as you cannot do anything with darkness. You can do something only with light. If you want to bring in light, you have to switch it on. If you have to bring in darkness, you have to switch off the light. Because darkness has no existence of its own, you cannot do anything with darkness. Darkness is there by default, the absence of light. Light is the reality. So whatever you have to do is to be done with reality.

So to kill desire, the desirer has to be killed. The desirer has to go. And the desirer can go only through consciousness. Because getting in touch with reality is an inside job. Alcohol, cigarettes, pill popping and playing the stock market are all just an external confirmation or compensation of your worthiness.

Envisage the Chase Maze as a circle. We may feel we are in the circle and accept we are in it but we are not aware of the centre. For us the centre cannot exist, because we cannot see it. We can only be there. From this point, we feel we are rising, but in reality we go around in circles. The circle is also moving and so we are never climbing, we are just moving while in the same spot, like on a treadmill. We are not smoking, we are being smoked; we are not consuming the junk food, we are actually getting consumed by it. You are not using money, the money is using you.

You can attain the centre by subscribing to infinity, by getting centred and not going around in circles. Because the circle is a constant thing, there is no stopping it. A man went to a seer and said, 'I'm tired of life running hither and thither, tell me which direction to go, I don't know which direction to go. And the seer said, stop, and just be; your path will be there.'

We want instant gratification instead of long-term results. We want to achieve the goals even before the process is over. We, therefore, lose out on the process. The whole participation in the process is lost. Not only is the essence of participation lost, the essence of the process is lost too. We are anxious about either winning or losing, lusting after it or craving it; you're greedy about it or you're fearful about it. And you're not living in the now, so you're losing it.

STOP. Drop chasing. Re-decide. Re-choose. Re-centre. Choose to be in the shoonya. Know your Shoonyam Quotient.

Get prioritized, get Mickeymized!

Shoonyam Quotient

4

'Man has a centre, but he lives off it—off the centre. That creates an inner tension, a constant turmoil, anguish. You are not where you should be; you are not at your right balance. You are off balance, and this being off balance, off centre, is the base of all mental tensions.

If it becomes too much, you go mad. A madman is one who has gone out of himself completely. The enlightened man is just the reverse of the madman. He is centred in himself.'

Osho, *The Book of Secrets*

Shoonyam Quotient is the measure of this centring.

Don't run away from life. Life is for living. One can't be complete by discarding or rejecting life. Enjoy it when it comes your way. Just be in a state of awareness. Stop yourself. Be in that awareness.

You are a part of more than one system at any given point of time. The Chase Maze is a meta-system of these systems all around you. You cannot avoid the system, nor am I advising you to do so. But can you go through it without getting affected by it? Once you become aware of the PH existence, once you look at the maze and understand that you are indeed running in it most of your life, you can look beyond it. To look beyond it, you don't even have to step out of it. You can just be still wherever you are in your life and rise.

STOP. LOOK. BECOME AWARE. BE AWARE. BE!

It's simple. For as long as possible in your day, as much as possible in your life, be aware. Be harmonized, be centred, accept life as it is and come out with an appropriate response. Just BE; and in your inaction–action, the appropriate response will emerge.

BE totally present to the space that you are in, BE totally there in the moment, BE in the here–now. Totality in the here–now creates absolute moments of limitless duration. BE one with the action that you are doing, the thought that you are thinking, the words that you are uttering—and you will find your Shoonyam Quotient.

Your HERE–NOW is the ONLY potential field for manifestation. If you are not total in that here–now, you have missed out. And how can you not be total? I will repeat myself, so it sinks in. In your here–now, if you are thinking about the past or reflecting on that past, you are not total. Or else, projecting your past into the future or planning and scheming about the future, again you are not total. You are missing out on your here–now completely. And that is your separation from your Shoonyam Quotient.

Getting to Shoonyam, the zero, and to the zero state sounds simple, but it is very difficult. At the same time, once you do it, once you are in the being and becoming through it, life becomes a breeze.

Shoonyam is the centre. And central in it is the source of all manifestation, which cannot be bounded, cannot be expressed, cannot be quantified and cannot be measured. The potential from there to become anything is vast; the potential to transform into anything is boundless.

Look at zero. It allowed humans to understand the concept of infinity. For centuries, calculations were done with digits from 1 to 9. Aryabhata introduced the concept of zero, saying that if we are unable to calculate something, it does not mean everything is finite. And we cannot represent or deal with infinity until we have dealt with zero. The whole universe is infinite and the energy that is spawning this, the energy that is weaving the whole universe with one thread, is infinite. He used zero—Shoonyam—to bring this infinity to the fore.

If you put zero against one, the value of zero becomes nine. If you put two zeroes against one, the value of zeroes becomes ninety-nine, ad infinitum. But most importantly, it is when you divide anything by zero that you get infinity mathematically.

$$X/0 = \text{Infinity}$$

Look at it another way. If you divide something by zero, you are actually not dividing it, but doing something even bigger. You are tapping into the infinity of its potential. When you divide something by one, the answer is the same. Symbolically, you have been able to tune into the manifest reality of it—the reality that is obvious and left untouched by one. On the other hand, the smaller the denominator and the smaller the base, the bigger the results. The closer you get to zero, the more you tune into the infinity, which is the ultimate potential, the real wholeness. You cannot get to infinity without the help of zero, as this equation shows. It is here that zero and infinity emerge as the two faces of the same reality. Zero is the base for getting to infinity.

When the force of creativity decided to become manifest, it split into the positive and the negative. Both came out of zero, and then kept on going until infinity. Retrieving from it is also the same. As Prabhupad points out, 'dhara' is that which goes out, 'radha' is that which comes in. It's the cycle from oneness to multiplicity, infinity, and then back to oneness again. Consciousness can never be plural; it is always one.

In terms of metaphysics and quantum physics, the zero state can be thought of as the alpha level wherein your mind is completely empty and only filled with light and the vibrancy of creation, which means *ved*— energy and information.

'Ved' means vibration of light. It means the creative energy that has created everything. Anything and everything that is manifested is made of ved. This energy of the ved is called *Ved Urja* (not to be confused with the Vedas or Vedanta—the former now means the ancient scriptures of India, and the latter, post-Vedic philosophy and inquiry into the Upanishads).

Ved is the basic energy. It is the source. We all have emanated from light and continue to be the creatures of light.

At first, there was light. And what is light? It is nothing but photons. We are beings of light, a light that can vibrate along with sound and can radiate.

This may sound strange, even downright stupid to you, unless you have experienced it yourself. Because that is the reality of energy. And it can be experienced very simply. You don't have to go out and look out for light. Just sit down and say, 'Aaa-oooo-mmmmm' . . . Integrating your mind, body and soul creates that light in you. On the screen of your consciousness, you will find a golden glow coming naturally, of its own accord. It will be a light that vibrates and a sound that radiates. You have to go into the state of Shoonyam. And for that, you have to empty the mind and just be a witness; you have to just watch without judgement or attachment.

At the very basic level, the two energies, light and sound, are also the same. They just manifest in different forms, either as sound or light. Rather, the energy gets perceived by us in those two distinct forms. That is the reason one could either have a vision or an intuition, in the states of surpassing conditioned perceptions; in the state that is pure consciousness.

Scientists have been studying consciousness for some time now. They have set up elaborate experiments and come up with findings that baffle them. For a long time, scientists thought that they were objective and were outside the system while observing it. And that is why they were intrigued by the findings. Gradually, it started dawning on the scientific community that however hard they try to step out of an observation, they cannot. And this paradigm shift brought about a quantum jump (quite literally as well) in their understanding. An observer can never be out of the system simply because they are both contained in the same seed. One can observe from the inside, but it would be a false assumption to believe that one can observe any event or activity from the outside. The only solution is thus dissolution—the observer and the observed becoming one, both dissolving in the seed.

Getting to Shoonyam is getting to that seed in which we are all contained. Because that is all there is.

The whole of the *brahmand*—the cosmos—is in you. You are the micro of the macro. As the universe, you are made of the five *tatvas*—or the five elements— earth, water, fire, sky and ether. You have them inside you. You cannot say which is which. You are them and they are you. The sun and the moon are in you in the form of the heat and the cold. The matter that you perceive outside is also the matter inside you. The gases are in you, the fluid is in you, the space is in you.

And yet, there is more than just these elements inside you. There is Memory. If you look at it materially, you can't pinpoint where memory is. So where does memory come from?

Memory is in the spaces. And however good we may feel about our ability to understand matter, we hardly understand the structure, nature and power of empty space. Even to know matter, you have to look at the spaces in between. Let's start looking at the spaces then. And strike a relationship with them as a step in the direction to understanding them.

Look around you: do you live in the walls, the floor or the ceiling? No, you live in the space contained in the walls. Once you start appreciating the spaces and not the matter, you will automatically start appreciating the hollowness of the matter itself.

Instead of just reading about it, here's how you can experience it: lie down and calm yourself to discover and deepen your relationship with the empty space. Start observing your breath. Don't make any conscious attempts to alter your breath, just observe it as it comes in and goes out. Suddenly, you will come to a viewing point where you are watching your body breathe. The separation will emerge: you and your breath. And if you and your breath are separate, then you will start appreciating that you are not your body.

Next, go on to observe your thoughts. Again, the separation will emerge: you and your thoughts. You will see that it is your mind that is thinking the thought. When you observe your mind, you will realize that you are not having these thoughts, your mind is, and you will say, 'This means I'm not this mind. I'm beyond this.'

What will start dawning upon you is the sense of the empty space, the emptiness, the wholeness—and the Shoonyam Quotient will be unveiled.

Lie down and quieten yourself
Start observing your breath

Observe it as it comes in and goes out

Watch your body breathe

Watch the separation: you and your breath

Watch the separation: you and your body

Start observing your thoughts

Observe as thoughts arise and disappear, one
leading to another

Watch the separation: you and your thoughts

Watch the separation: you and your mind

Observe the sense of the empty space, the emptiness,
the wholeness . . .

BE in the SHOONYAM

BE the SHOONYAM

So if you are not your body and not your mind, who, or
rather, what, are you? You are what your reality is in
space. You have stemmed from here. And rejuvenation
can happen only at this point. And this process of
centring is a process to bring you into balance—from
the periphery of the circle of life to the centre of it.
The more you centre yourself throughout the day, the
more habitual it becomes. Finally, there comes a point
in time when you are centred 24x7.

Whenever an experience remains unfulfilled, you
are not wholesome, you are not total, you are not
satiated. You collect experiences, the experiences
become memory and memory creates a desire for
more such experiences. (In the case of a painful or a
discomforting experience, memory creates a desire for
not having the experience ever again, but it is a desire
nonetheless.) But if you are total, completely satiated

within the experience, then the desire is completely dissolved. For, with satiation comes freedom from experience. Then there is no memory significant enough to create an action towards it.

When there is no desire, there is no significant build-up of memory that will haunt you. It will not become an obsession because nothing is repressed there.

Like I mentioned before, when you are having sex and you are simultaneously thinking of many other things, then you are never fulfilled with sex and you become obsessed with it.

It is the same with food.

When this desire–memory cycle, is broken, the only consequence is that you are free. Deliverance from this cycle makes you arrive at pure action. All your life you are driven by memory and desire. Then comes the state when your actions are free of these, and this is when you attain moksha, liberation.

Because desires and memories constantly seek manifestation, you constantly make choices and never become choice-less. Unless you become choice-less, you remain incomplete. If you are making a choice, it simply means that for you there is still something left to seek. It keeps you from a space where there is inaction in action.

And even for the choices that you wish to manifest, you have to remember that in your being and becoming is your co-operation with life, not the interruption of the process. When you are reflected by memory and driven by desire, you are interfering with the process of manifestation, because manifestation happens when you give it time and space, when there is discontinuity and a mutation of consciousness. It is facilitated by the space given to it. Manifestation gets a chance by the space given to it. When you look at a clock constantly, it tends to appear as if it has slowed down. So don't monitor your life, don't watch it with intention.

If you wish to manifest, watch it being intention-less, view-less, desire-less and opinion-less. And that watching will be your transformational vertex, the point of transformation, the point of alchemy. At that point, you can change anything.

According to Osho, we have all experienced being away from our centres. We have been through our moments of extreme anxiety, anger or cravings, which are the glimpses of our being away from our centres. Similarly, we have all tasted the centring in the form of those relaxed moments when everything has fitted perfectly and the world seems a perfect place to be in. When you are in love or when you are at a beautiful place, when you are with your dear ones or when you have had a good workout, you have touched the centre and have also stayed in it. What you always wanted is alive for you then. Where you wanted to be, you have reached (or it has reached you) and there is a stop, a gap, in your thought.

But, both of these, centring and being away from it, have remained fleeting extremes. So fleeting that most of the time you only remember them in the past. The centre, however, is our true home. That's where we get the feeling of staying, the feeling of being. There is no craving or a pull to go anywhere, as it seems like the completion of a journey. It is in Shoonyam that you are the real you—calm, composed, relaxed. There are no ambitions to achieve, no stress to deal with. You are effortlessly there. Your being is all that there is. There is only being and no becoming. You are in the moment all the time. Life becomes a series of present moments, of continuous here–nows. Neither the past nor the future governs you. All your actions arise from the here–now and not from any craving or desires.

When you are in Shoonyam, your life is neither an extension of the past nor a projection of the future. For instance, if you are exercising in Shoonyam, you are neither doing it with thoughts of your heart condition, which prompted you to take up exercising in the first place, nor are you concerned with the thoughts of how good you will look the next week. When you are exercising, you are only exercising.

These are the moments of transformation, no matter how small they may seem. In those rare moments, you feel altered. It is this change that I am talking about. If those infrequent moments can bring about the glimpses of transformation, imagine the transformational vertex you will touch when you stay in that centre for longer and longer, or even forever.

Now look at what happens when thoughts inundate you while you are exercising. Instead of exercising, you are more interested in the outcome of it. You want to have a particular figure or physique within a month. The quality of the exercise suffers as becoming is more important than doing. And even if one desire gets completed, how long is it before the next one starts troubling you. If you entertain one thought, your mind will not stop there. It will keep jumping from this one to the next, and the next.

The irony is that our insecurities follow us even to the moments of thought-lessness, and we start worrying if the same state would continue in the next moment. We start thinking—will the same scenery be available to me once I leave this place? Will he call me back at all? Will this figure remain if I am unable to exercise tomorrow? Or when I grow old?

One who lives off the Shoonyam is always pulled from all sides and their life is a constant fluctuation from one reality to another, from one thought to another. On the other hand, when you are in the here–now, in pure action, there is only being and no becoming. Such is the time that you are totally into yourself, centred. In fact, you are the centre, the empty, the whole . . . the Shoonyam.

Once you are attached to the outcome of your doing, you are either anxious and fearful about it or ambitious and greedy about it. In both these conditions, you are bound to make mistakes. Bound to meet disaster. And in both you are not total in the act. If you are detached both from the outcome of winning and losing, but are total in it, taking whatever comes out of it as the appropriate outcome, you will enjoy the process. And in that enjoyment of the process is the experience you collect of the transformation. That experience itself will transform you. And that is the point where the experience, the experiencer and the process of experiencing are one. They are not separate.

There is wholeness, there is bliss. There is no happiness, no sadness, no joy and no suffering. There is pure bliss. That is being centred.

That means one is neither happy nor sad nor upset. One is just watching. In a nutshell, there is wholeness, the essence of wholeness, the centre of consciousness. What does that mean to an objective mind? It means integration. Integration of mind, body and soul and becoming complete. From doing to being!

Now that we have looked at why being whole or complete is essential, immediately the next query arises: what concrete steps does one take to get to this Shoonyam Quotient? What is it practically that will make me so?

We need to look at and integrate all the areas of our lives. Not just the waking lives, but our sleep and the state beyond sleeping as well. And we can arouse the Shoonyam Quotient for each of the areas. We need to get down to something as practical as sleeping at the right hours, exercising every day, breathing, meditating and introspecting every day, having the appropriate food the appropriate way, and thinking about how these steps will lead us to further integration.

Shoonyam Quotient is to be developed and honed when you are eating, when you are breathing, when you are resting, making love, in a relationship—at every point, circumstance or situation. It is simply how you are centred in that situation. And how that centring is creating the wholeness, completeness. For example, wholeness in the process of eating arises from the appropriate type of food, the way of eating and the aptness of time. Completeness in exercise blooms through mindfulness and deep compassion for the specific part being exercised. In essence, all the areas of your life get centred and eventually harmonize into your life.

The Shoonyam Quotient is experiential and subjective. It can get better and better; there is no ceiling to it. Eventually, this quotient reaches the level where nothing makes a difference to you, and you live life with 100 per cent witness value—between the polarities of life, where the pendulum of your existence stops oscillating between past and future. It is very personal and individualistic, and thus, non-comparable. You can read and hear descriptions of it, but its uniqueness is specific to you alone, and will become yours only when you yourself experience it. You cannot quantify it, but can adjudge your Shoonyam Quotient from the personal experience of displacement from it, in the form of any anxiety, stress or anger you have. Once you have arrived at it, you are Shoonyam . . . there is no Quotient.

This is an attempt to simplify your life. And though the experience of Shoonyam could first occur in that manner, it should not be thought of as an injunction to deny anything to yourself. It doesn't say don't go and watch a movie. Only that when you do, do it in complete harmony. There are no problems left in that simplicity. The bottom line is to harmonize your being and becoming. There is no disturbance, distortion or imbalance in your being and becoming, the balance being super dynamic.

You can do that with your food, your work, or rest. If you do that during the day, then you are a centred person and you have holistic health. What is being recommended is health beyond fitness. The word health is derived from the Greek 'heal' and it means to heal from within. Do nothing from the outside. Just be the facilitator for your body to work for itself. If you want any kind of transformation, just be. When you just BE, you are meeting and uniting with the source. Everything is available there—all creativity, intelligence, organizing ability, health, spiritual power and dynamism. The throbbing here–now, the pulsating here–now, which means the sound and the light, is available there. We are nothing but the beings of light. So in that we can be illuminated.

This centre of existence has no beginning, middle or end, since it was never born and it will never die. It is time-less and space-less, which means it has no location in space and no moment in time.

When I am training my clients, whether personal clients or those for beauty pageants, this is what I try to inculcate in them—no short-term application of external supplements but going inwards and bringing out the infinite beauty, grace and health inherent in each one of us. For instance, I do not recommend fast weight loss as it brings about energy imbalance and hormonal imbalance.

My process would be to start at the gross level, detoxifying yourself, changing your attitude, your behavioural pattern to bring out the woman or man of substance, who is nothing but love: unconditional love, unconditional benevolence, unconditional philanthropy and unconditional strength. The choice to be a crown winner or a dynamic mother after that is just a matter of an effortless step.

It is difficult to understand the Shoonyam because it is uncountable. We have conditioned ourselves to understand only the countables. More importantly, we have an almost obsessive need to 'understand' everything. Here is an invitation to go beyond this need. To take a dip in the Shoonyam. This dip nourishes your pure being-ness like the usual three meals are supposed to nourish your body.

Ask yourself this vital question:

Have you taken your Shoonyam dip today?

Get neutralized, get Mickeymized!

Polarities

5

All in the world recognize the beautiful as beautiful.
Herein lies ugliness.
All recognize the good as good.
Herein lies evil.
Therefore, being and non-being produce each other.
Difficulty and ease bring about each other.
Long and short delimit each other.
High and low rest on each other.
Sound and voice harmonize each other.
Front and back follow each other.
Therefore, the sage abides in the condition of *wu-wei*
(unattached action).
And carries out the wordless teaching.
Here, the myriad things are made, yet not separated.
Therefore, the sage produces without possessing,
Acts without expectations and accomplishes without
abiding in her accomplishments.
It is precisely because she does not abide in them
that they never leave her.

—Lao Tzu
Tao Te Ching

There is no different 'I' other than the whole universe itself. All of this creation is contained in you. What is contained inside you is not just what is there in the present, but also all that ever was and can ever be. You were never born and you will never die. However difficult it may be for you to accept it and confirm this using the tests you use to define the reality of your life, you are eternity in entirety. The polarities that you experience arise from you being just the reflection of the polarities existing in the universe.

The universe does exist in polarities. There are polarities in the outside world and the inside world, and there are different ways in which we deal with these polarities. We often simply ignore them. We experience them, but in a way that the other polarity is ignored. At times, we suffer and become resigned to this game of God and question why he or she had to make the other polarity.

We wonder how happy and wonderful life would be if there was only one good extreme after another. That is actually like saying how wonderful it would be if there were only mountains and no valleys. A mountain cannot exist without a valley beside it. In a human being, good and bad coexist. The saint and the sinner both make their presence felt together. And at times, we just become scared of this game of polarities and stop living life fully.

From one extreme to another, a human being keeps oscillating. And it is not so in all the polarities. There are certain opposites that one is not even aware of. And there are others that one is aware of, but only at a surface level. For instance, happiness and grief. We always want to be happy and avoid being sad. And when something causes grief, we suffer. Now there is nothing wrong with grief, but all our life is spent in avoiding it. Moreover, it is rarely that we realize that happiness and grief are actually just responses, having no external existence outside us.

The very first step to diffuse polarities is to become aware of them and their cyclical pattern. And then diffuse them in the Shoonyam state. The element of perfect balance and harmony is what makes one attain Shoonyam, where one lives spontaneously, in the present always without thinking; in unbounded consciousness. Even the so-called saints tend to conduct themselves with the virtue of subtle greed and the desire of being rewarded with heaven and the upliftment of their souls.

Polarities give the illusion of life. Working sixteen hours a day, partying all night on Saturdays till the next morning and sleeping for the next fifteen hours is living that kind of polarity. We skip our meals at work, and then binge eat later. We starve ourselves for weeks following the new diet fad and spend the next six months gorging on all the junk food. People living in polarities would say: 'Come on! What would life be if there were no polarities . . . If there were no ups and downs?' Not only do we indulge, entertain and tolerate such things ourselves, but also make some kind of religion out of it.

Balancing does not mean that there will be no ups and downs in your life. It's your relationship with them that will undergo a sea change when you start getting centred. You will be able to transcend those experiences and not collect them. And when you stop collecting them, they will automatically stop perpetuating in your life. As an obvious side effect, the recurring patterns of your life, like the fluctuations in your emotional life, will also fade away.

When you are in the centre, you are anchored without being cemented. You are loose without drifting. You have a 360-degree perception without being biased or confused. So when you are at the centre, it may seem that you are drifting, but you are surely anchored. Though it appears that you are not cemented, you are actually so. However, when you are at the periphery, it appears that you are cemented but you are not. It may seem like you are dull in the centre but you are rooted . . . completely rooted. You may look extra cautious but you are just alert. Firm, but not harsh, soft but not yielding.

When in the centre, you may seem not to be in control, but you are in full control. While on the outside, just the opposite is true. You seem fixed but you are drifting.

In the Bhagavadgita, Krishna says to Arjun, *sukh-dukhe same kritva labha labhau jaya jayau*. In the ultimate treatise on polarity, Krishna urges Arjun to treat the polarities of happiness and grief, profit and loss, glory and shame as equal, and then fight. He never once said that these polarities did not exist. He was making Arjun realize the futility of attaching too much meaning to these, because they are in effect two faces of the same coin. If one is visible, the other can't be hidden for long. The wise Krishna says, see both together and never in isolation.

Lao-tzu also talks of wordless teaching and unattached action. Unattached action is not action devoid of energy or spirit. It is just an action devoid of expectation. And that happens only after the true nature of these polarities is understood. Lao-tzu says if you entertain a polarity or make it significant, immediately the other extreme of it is born. As soon as you call an action good, you have, in effect, given birth to what would be bad action. No sooner have you appreciated one painting as good, you have made a lot of others ugly. Because in the same moment as the creation of this category, 'good', the other category, 'bad', is also born. A wise man, thus, often stays silent.

Shoonyam is like the axle of a wheel, which doesn't move but everything around it moves and everything moves around it! The Shoonyam state is the centre around which the polarities move, but do not affect it.

The ultimate polarity is the polarity of space–time. Your mind is always wandering to past experiences or future expectations. Thoughts are perpetually travelling from one place to another, travelling to destinations all over the globe in a matter of seconds. If you look closely, all the polarities of your experiential world manifest on this space–time continuum, and once you have centred yourself here, all the polarities are taken care of by themselves.

THE POLARITIES MEDITATION

Sit down in a comfortable position.

Observe your thoughts.

Is the thought coming from the past?

If it is, just observe it and drop it.

Choose to be in this moment.

Is the thought coming from the future?

If it is, just observe it and drop it.

Choose to be in this moment.

Is the thought about some other place than this?

If it is, just observe it and drop it.

Choose to be only here.

Choose to be in the here–now.

Get equalized, get Mickeymized!

Sleep vis-à-vis Rejuvenating Rest

6

When you are tired, you need to rest. When you are done with your days' worth of doing and thinking, you need rest. We can look at our lives and say, there are times when we live and at other times, we rest. We could say there are times when we live—doing, thinking or being a certain way. Or involved in the madness—the madness of polarities, almost like the futile exercise of building a sandcastle to be destroyed by the next wave coming in, wondering why we built the castle in the first place. The madness of doing and undoing, digging and filling, and, at other times, resting.

For us, it is our life vis-à-vis rest. But, in actuality, it is the rest of our life or the other part of our life. And that is why how you are in the other parts affects the rest of your life.

Sleep is the only way for our bodies to get maximum rest. Or the maximum amount of rest we are supposed to get. Even though we say, 'I'm going to get some sleep' or 'I had a good sleep', in reality, it's the sleep that gets us and has us. After a good day's work, all one wants is to do is 'hit the sack'.

And how beautiful it would be if it were as simple as getting tired, going to sleep and waking up refreshed. Sleep-related disorders are the first to crop up when the Shoonyam Quotient is lost. One either doesn't sleep enough or doesn't feel rested after a long night's sleep. It is rest—and not sleep, however many hours of it—that is important.

All of our waking hours are filled with thoughts, actions and words. And behind all of this lies the constant magnetic pull of polarities. This pull is erratic; sometimes it draws us to the extreme polarity and sometimes only half-draws us towards it. The intentions or desires, the experiences and the memories keep perpetuating more desires, more thoughts and more memories, taking us from one polarity to the next. It is when we sleep (or are forced to sleep) that there is some semblance of tuning into pure intention and thought-lessness.

It is a submission, a mechanism of the mind to take respite from our constant swinging between polarities. But it is not always that sleep is a respite. The swinging is taken to bed, at times by conscious worries and at other times through suppressed, unattended anxieties. And so you miss the Shoonyam Quotient of sleep, the rejuvenating rest.

One should be so total throughout the day that eventually your body, your existence, just surrenders. A surrender in which one feels no sense of loss or regret because nothing is incomplete, nothing is carried as baggage, so there are no thoughts haunting you or disturbing you. A surrender in which there is no struggle because nothing is being carried forward, whose loss would generate a resistance or regret.

A Paranoid Humanoid, however, would be up in arms at this assertion. She would tell the next PH, 'I fall into bed like a dead horse and sleep deeply till the bloody alarm goes off.' Unaware sleep, deep sleep, rejuvenating sleep and rest—how we have forgotten how to distinguish between them. To counter the insomnia caused by our greedy existence and the paranoia and anxieties generated by it, we actually tire ourselves to the bone (or to the last neuron, if we fancy ourselves to be those who work with our brains). Exhausting ourselves, deliberately or subconsciously, is the formula we use to fall asleep. The next time you hear an alarm, let it be an alarm to alert you that you have forgotten the distinction between sleep and rejuvenating rest.

Sleep can provide only physical rest and that too to a very limited extent. More likely, it has just become a mechanism your system uses to switch itself off in a desperate attempt to prevent further self-abuse. It is more like an auto function where you can't keep your eyes open any more.

There are also times, more frequent than not, when a PH takes stimulants to keep awake. Cuppas and cuppas of coffee to make him stay awake to study or meet work deadlines. And, at other times, the same people need to read to sleep!

Why doesn't anyone ever think of staying in bed by oneself to enjoy it completely: to enjoy the pillow, to enjoy the feel of the bed sheets, to enjoy your even breath, to enjoy your relaxed body lying in bed. Just being calm, delving deeper and deeper inside oneself. Why can't you do that? Why are you so afraid of being alone with yourself? Why do people have to run away from emptiness?

Sleep is a mechanical process as long as it does not recharge you. If you are merely sleeping and not feeling rested, if the rest is not rejuvenating you, then you are displaced from your Shoonyam Quotient of sleep.

Rest itself can be defined in three aspects—physically, psychologically and spiritually. Only then will you be completely rested. In any other case, even if you have slept for twelve hours, you will wake up tired. On the other hand, when you rest with these three components, you wake up calm and fresh. How you derive the Shoonyam Quotient through rest is important. Because all this integrates you.

If you are well rested in your sleep, your mental frequencies come down to Shoonyam. In such a state, your brain is not thinking, dreaming or doing calculations. In this case, when you get up even after only two hours of sleep, you feel fresh. Freshness comes only after the muting of clinical consciousness. Rest is supposed to bring you there, where the brain comes to its lowest frequency.

Before you sleep, cleanse yourself thoroughly to have a rejuvenating rest. Be physically clean, have a bath, brush your teeth, gargle and then cleanse yourself psychologically. You can drop all that you have been carrying as burden all through the day, maybe even all your life. As soon as you realize that you are carrying something, it is the best time to drop it. Generate a sense of gratitude for all that you can be thankful for—in your life and in your world. Seek redemption for yourself, for all your transgressions, and forgive all who have trespassed against you. Have the full attention of your body and relax it completely. Submit yourself completely to the Shoonyam of rejuvenating rest.

GETTING YOUR REJUVENATING REST

Be clean when ready to sleep.

Lie down on your bed and make yourself comfortable.

Observe your body.

Become aware of each part of your body starting from the toes to the top of your head.

Relax each part as you become aware of it.

Relax your whole body.

Observe your thoughts.

Thank life and the creator for all that you can.

Say in your mind, 'I forgive you unconditionally.'

Take in a deep breath and gently release it.

Say in your mind, 'I forgive myself unconditionally.'

Take in a deep breath and gently release it.

Say in your mind, 'I let go completely.'

Take in a deep breath and gently release it.

Say in your mind, 'I submit myself completely.'

Let yourself sink into the rejuvenating rest.

Get energized, get Mickeymized!

Superstitions and Entrapments

7

In the aware state of being, one taps into unbounded consciousness, is absolutely alert and always responds to life appropriately; whereas in the entrapped psychological state, one is lost in the process of thinking, caught unawares by the flow of life and is thus prone to accidents, disasters and catastrophes. Transformation can lead to transcendence, which is nothing but evolution.

There are different levels of superstitions that we subscribe to. From the downright ridiculous (ridiculous for one and sacrosanct for another), to the elaborate and the esoteric, covering all the rigid and axiomatic beliefs, and all the belief systems in between. How can one ever find out the truth, the real truth, the absolute truth? Can there be any other way but to drop all that is known and turn inward to let the truth reveal itself? Instead, what we subscribe to are the biggest lies and we become their victims. And then we subscribe to quick fixes and entrapments to deal with this victimhood. The journey of transformation is the journey of how a victim of entrapment becomes a victor of enlightenment.

For instance, you may receive a mail or SMS containing a prayer. The message also enumerates the good things that will come to you if you forward it to eight people, and what the consequences of deleting it will be. One side of the story is the business that it generates for the network company, which must have generated it in the first place. Say, in the beginning, it was sent to 100 people, each one of whom sends it to eight people. So it has reached 800 people and then each one of them sends it to eight more people. Some will send it to even more people, some to fewer people and some to none at all; but, on an average, it will get sent, increasing its reach in geometrical proportions.

Another aspect is the archetypal energy involved, like that of a gemstone. We devote a lot of attention, focus, time and energy to it. We place a lot of faith, love, hope and trust in it. If we conform to the unified field of energy theory and its laws, this is also a part of it. When we are adding energy to it or putting energy into it, this energy is bound to get reflected back into the system. That is how gems, artefacts, pendants and charms work. Maybe this is how chain SMSes and mails also seem to work.

Like the gemstone, even the chain SMS contains the faith, hope, love and trust of people through whom it has come to you. Now, say you are reading it without any scepticism. You read it in pure faith, not considering the motives that lie behind this chain or the thought of forwarding it. You just read it with pure faith and send it to more people in pure faith. The whole message gets stronger and stronger. The eight angel's factor, as recognized in the mystical streams of Abrahamic religions, becomes your archetypal energy, because it is within the energy circulating in those people.

And maybe some people who have generated it have done it for their own limited purpose, others out of fear, some just did it for the sake of doing it and some do it out of love. Many people start putting energy into it and it reaches you.

Now comes the question of entrapment. If you are doing this out of fear, then it is an entrapment. And if you're acting out of love or compassion, it becomes an indication of nature to return it.

If somebody insults me, and I say out of love, 'It is an interesting remark', that means I'm free. Free of the cycle that a word would have set in motion. Free from the compulsion to try in vain to balance the order of my dignity. (Whereas, it was never out of order in the first place!)

Here also, the objectivity and the subjectivity involved make it a matter of freedom, and you have a choice. Not that you are bound, but that you are doing something out of love makes it an integral part of your being. In that part of your being, this message has come to you. Your action in inaction has brought it about and not because you did it as a good deed prescribed in some text.

That goes for all archetypal energies—including gems, stones, colours, etc.

The beautiful truth driving this cosmos and everything contained in it is that everything is possible. Everything is possible and nothing is certain. This gives an opportunity to drop fears and manifest the higher self that lies inside you. Everything else is plain and simple superstition, arising from the fundamental superstition—I am a victim.

Superstitions are the fodder for all our illusions. A superstition is a mental construct; piled up, heaped up memories and perceptions, interpretations coming from a bundle of conditioned reflexes. Such reactions take us away from the flow of life, because superstitions always create escapism. For example, if a cat cuts across your path, then don't walk ahead on that path. Who knows if that very road might lead to your own El Dorado! On that route, your deliverance might be awaiting you. And what one thinks of as an accident lurking to pounce on you might just be the premonition of it. And we want to avoid that possible accident that may or may not happen.

Now, that accident is possible. Maybe the cat crosses your path and you meet with an accident. But that accident is your pathway on your very unique journey to salvation. The human mind thinks of only one instance or a chain of such events in isolation. It will not see the picture in totality. For the person who sees the picture in totality, superstitions don't exist.

Superstitions are isolated phenomena, not interrelated, not interconnected, not part of an orchestra. They are a partial vision of life, developed out of belief systems and the law of averages. Say five out of ten people have been affected; so it did cause something bad. Even if something bad happens to two people, it will be highlighted, but that nothing happened to the other eight will be ignored. The human mind wants to find a pattern in things. Even in things that don't have any pattern. There is a great desire for creative expression, which gets translated in these instances when no alternative outlet for this energy exists. That's ingrained in human nature. The next automatic step is to subscribe to, anticipate and finally enact the same pattern.

You will find whatever you seek in this universe; that is inherent in its blue print. What is ingrained in human nature and intrinsic to the blueprint of the universe finds an exact fit in the entrapment.

That's why, entrapment. Again, this comes about when there is separation. Senses, thinking, logic, interrelation, all play havoc under the fear-driven thought, 'Why take a chance if it has happened to others? Better to be safe than sorry.'

A complete person, a whole person, will not be affected by *vaastu* and feng shui, palmistry and planetary movement, charms and spirits. And it's not that there are no pluses and minuses in the state of wholesomeness. Even in the state of wholesomeness, there are pluses and minuses, but if there is an excess of anything, it flows out, and if there is a deficiency or lack, it flows in. If there is excess energy, it will be discharged and if the energy is lacking, it will be absorbed. Such a state is an invincible state . . . Wherein you let yourself be vulnerable, but you are not vulnerable . . . And so you are beyond the reach of vaastu, feng shui, etc.

As long as you are not whole, you have to keep adding the supplements of information, knowledge, dictates and constructs. There is no harm in using these supplements but there is also the loss of freedom over time as the dependence increases and the entrapment becomes bigger and deeper.

Does that mean a centred man is beyond nature? Well, it actually means that the centred man *is* nature! At some level, the distance between the Creator and the created is dissolved. Here, it is not matter, but the essence—the spirit that is in discussion. It is the ultimate spirit that will be beyond the state of suffering and trauma. It will always be ever-expanding. On and on, physically also it will be more and more profound. It will be consolidated.

The nature of matter is that it has to eventually break down. And reunite with its source—that is energy. That which is indestructible is energy. There is information that binds and directs this energy. Matter is destructible.

The effect of the spirit envelopes the body and shows through it too. Eastern mystics, the yogis, have demonstrated it umpteen times. Eventually, even if the soul has to leave a body, it will leave a profound effect on the body. Swami Yogananda Paramahansa, one of the best-known eastern mystics, demonstrated this phenomenon elegantly. His body was untouched by bacteria for twenty-one days after his death. It remained warm for hours after he died. It did not smell for weeks together; it did not decompose. Imagine the kind of refinement it must have attained. It defied all that was known about the state of the human body after death and pushed all that knowledge into the domain of superstition.

At the matter level, there is super-determinism. At this level, everything that has to support matter will support matter. That can be one level of existence. There is another level that is possible, however.

The gems or the charms that one would use are not taking you away from entrapment. They are taking you deeper into it. It's the kind of knowledge that is robbing you of the truth, taking you farther from it.

Then, there are the next levels of superstitions, which have been born out of the fertility of the human mind working in the areas of science, politics and religion. It would not be unfair to call science the modern superstition, going by the realizations that the scientific community itself has been having in recent times. Half of all that was considered the victory of mankind till very recently, such as the atom bomb, has unequivocally been accepted as a mistake. The other half, such as vaccination and the Newtonian system of cause and effect, is under close scrutiny as we talk about it. At the core of these superstitions is simply the absence of a holistic outlook. From the collective to the individual, the one big question is: how can the mind be aroused to get the total picture?

If you look straight ahead, steadily, you will have a 180-degree view. If you move your eyeballs to the right, you get the view of the right side. If you move your eyeballs to the left side, you see that side. The total picture is in the centre. So it is with the mind. You move your mind to the past—you get a partial picture. You move it to the future—again, it's a partial picture. You move it to any specific place or thought; you see an illusion, an essence, a partial picture or a distorted picture. In the here–now, there is a complete picture.

If you were to perceive anything with all your senses, you would get a complete picture. All your senses need to get merged seamlessly. That is when it becomes pure consciousness. And it is not just the sum of all the senses, but something more than that, something beyond that.

There was a time when man thought the sun went around the earth. From the level that the sun went around the earth, right up to the level that man was supposed to grow old and die, the entire belief system was a spectrum of superstitions. And the reality is very different from facts and perceptions—man is supposed to renew with time and not wither away; one never grows old when one stops growing, one becomes old. Does that mean man is immortal? No. Man simply needs to transform, transmigrate. Death has no right on life—it is the culmination of your disease; disease is the culmination of your doing. At every given point in life, we can choose evolution over entropy.

In the light of awareness, nothing dies. All is life. Life is the only constant. In the awareness of life and light, nothing dies. Because living and dying is a part of every microsecond. One has to let their past die to keep living in the present moment and thus be eternal. Eternity comes here. Dying is a process. If you don't let every moment of the past die, you will not stay young. And if you keep dying in every moment of the past, you never grow old and even dying itself becomes just a process.

Truth is constant. Knowledge is not. Truth is what never changes. Knowledge keeps growing and changing. It is our relationship with truth that keeps changing with the changing knowledge. When we are not flexible enough to keep our relationship firm with the new form of truth that emerges, we face conflict. That is what psychologists call transference. Far worse is the situation when we subscribe to the knowledge that binds us instead of liberating us.

Superstitions are deductions from such knowledge and the truth inherent in them is as stable as the shifting sands. Nature keeps indicating through situations, circumstances and signals. Pick up the signals, but don't get affected by them. Maybe nature is trying to forewarn you. Maybe there is no indication at all. Both possibilities exist together because life is a co-existence. The ideal is to be . . . just be! Just be in the Shoonyam.

Don't react. Watch. In your watching with compassion comes your response to life, cooperation with life. It is then that you are being, and making the life be.

When you are not interfering with the process of manifestation, nothing will interfere with your process of manifestation. The smallest of your wishes will be fulfilled. The slightest of your thoughts and intentions will be manifested.

Get individualized, get Mickeymized!

Breathing vis-à-vis Aware-halation

8

Atman is the state of your soul. The soul is a bundle of Karmas. In Karmas there is no good or bad. Good or bad depends on your point of view. It is appropriate to the moment, circumstance and situation. In this situation, something could be right; in the next instance, the same thing could be wrong. The bottom line is that there is nothing right, nothing wrong; nothing white, nothing black; nothing hard and nothing soft. The Soul is untouched by the qualities of good, bad, hard and soft. At the level of the soul, everything is just one, there is one totality. If you subscribe to the idea of universality, wholeness, totality and integration, you are subscribing to the idea of eternity and then you are completely relaxed. There is no anxiety, no insecurity. There is no lust, greed, resentment, vengeance or phobia. You are calm and cool. You are in the centre, the Shoonyam.

Your centring begins from the realization, 'I'm not the body and I'm not the mind, but I'm the one with the body and the mind.' No sooner do you realize that you can watch your body breathe that you realize you can watch your thoughts. Thoughts keep coming and going. Do not get attached to them. Do not judge them, do not act ON them, do not react TO them. Just watch. Your thoughts are nothing but the being and becoming of millennia accumulated, because as of now you haven't reached the state of getting into that gap between thoughts. You are inundated with thoughts, billions of them floating in the universe. That's the collective consciousness—all your desires and collective desires, all your experiences and collective experiences, all your memories and collective memories. At the body level we appear to be separate, at the mind level we overlap, and at the soul level we are all one. We are all part of the one source; we come from there and go back to it.

When you watch your breath, you become aware that this is the life force. You appreciate it and watch with compassion. If there is only one quality that needs to be added to your watching, it is that of compassion. No sooner do you practice it, does selfishness exit and selflessness enter. In that selflessness, you are one, throbbing and pulsating with the whole universe, in that moment, in the here–now. You are alive.

You are alive in that moment, but your mind is not. Because when your mind is, you are not. And when your mind is not, you are. The mind is a phenomenon, the existence of which means you are either in the past or in the future. Your mind cannot exist in the present. The present is the light that your mind cannot stand.

In the here–now there is no thought. There is spontaneity. Thought exists when there is distance. In the here–now there is no distance, because there is no thought. In the here–now, there is no agenda. Nothing is cramped; it's just a flow. It's spontaneity. You are connected, you are one, you are whole.

And this wholeness is just emptiness. The emptiness pours itself infinitely. It is this emptiness that we call by different names—God, Almighty, Supreme Nature, Divine.

So what could be called emptiness could also be called hollowness and nothingness, and that is the absolute. This selfless absolute state is *anatma*, the state where you are free from desires, memories and experiences. With every act you do in this state, you don't collect the memory. So the memory doesn't engender a desire, and the desire doesn't drive you to do more action. You are not trapped in the vicious cycle.

If there is one thing that connects everything to everything, and anything to everything, it's our breath. Breath is the single most important component of life for all living beings. For the survival of the Earth and the living, oxygen is very important. We can do without water and food for days but we cannot do without breath for more than a few minutes.

The important thing is how we metabolize our breath. It is how we take it in, in quantities appropriate for our regeneration. Breath is connected primarily with our rejuvenation, recreation and revitalization. It is connected with our invigoration, renewal and most importantly, it keeps us ticking in balance. If inhalation and exhalation are in perfect harmony, forces of entropy cannot touch us.

All integration, all transcendence, all reality and realization of truths, can happen only when a breath has first been taken into your consciousness, into your awareness, into your process of being and becoming. Then it goes into a level of subtlety and refinement when you have not forgotten it, or become oblivious to it. It becomes so refined that with the least breathing you can live the longest.

At that level, the body has learnt to metabolize the smallest speck of breath that goes in. Oxygen that goes in can be retained for twenty hours or more. That's why the need for breath becomes so subtle, so refined. The need to take conscious deep breaths and fill the chest with more and more oxygen consciously disappears. Breathing becomes lighter and lighter, subtly filling the remotest pores with an abundance of oxygen.

The cycle of thoughts and manifestation is closely intertwined with your breath. Your breath directs your thoughts. When your intentions are introduced into this universe, and your breathing is normal, perfect, regulated, the manifestation of your thoughts also takes place in due course of time. You have laid the fundamental ground for manifestation, giving it time and space thereafter. It is like sowing the seed and allowing time and space to process it. Process the information and intention. Your thoughts, your intention, information and desire have to get processed. Breath can empower intention, empower thoughts and give you the strength to envelope the existence, the whole universe and universes. Breath can make you receive, perceive, pick up signals from others' mind, tune into the cosmic consciousness and make you pulsate with the pulse of this universe, every microsecond.

At the physical level, breathing is the oxygenation of the body. But all that breathing does is improve your stamina for carbon dioxide (CO_2) tolerance, which means how long you can tolerate CO_2 build-up in your body.

Your breath is so powerful that it can also make you get rid of physiological toxins from your body. You can cause them to evaporate just through your breath, by visualizing that they are getting dissolved with every breath you take.

You can breathe out and ease your entire psychological and emotional trauma. You can bring back the balance of tranquillity and bliss. Breath can get you centred once again. Breath can allow you to be collected, to be integrated, to put all the loose pieces together and set you on the path of regeneration from the path of degeneration. Breath brings you balance and equilibrium.

Yogic traditions call breath the '*praanvayu*', the carrier of the '*pranas*'. Watching your breath can tell you what state you are in. Once you develop this constant awareness of your breath coming slowly or fast, it can tell you what emotional state you are in. As soon as you are aware that your breath is out of order, you will be aware of your emotional state, and thus, that emotional state will immediately lose its power. The Shoonyam quotient of breath will emerge.

The process of getting to the Shoonyam quotient of the breath begins by watching it. Simply watching it come in and leave your body. Watch your body breathing. Watching is like light. In that light of watching, everything calms down, everything falls back into place, everything is salvaged, everything is restored and everything is healed. The more and more subtle you get, the more easily you start slipping into the gap. Because the gap between each breath becomes longer, every breath you breathe is utilized to its optimum efficiency. Not only that, but the other systems of your body also respond harmoniously.

All this accrues from the physiological and anatomical advantages of the hatha yoga discipline and then follows the universal level of breathing.

For someone who has never done any sort of pranayama or breathing exercises, the first thing is to have a consciousness of inhalation and exhalation. Then comes awareness of the external and internal retention of breath or the gap in the breaths.

First, for a few months, for as many times in the day as you can, become aware of your breath and use the mental applications on it. Before eating, after eating and while eating, before drinking anything, after drinking and while drinking, whenever emotional traumas, mental traumas, physical pains and psychological pains bother you—just get into a conscious breathing pattern. Take a deep breath in and a deep breath out. Don't count the breath or try to hold it. Just breathe in and breathe out. Breathe in strength, breathe out weakness; breathe in joy, breathe out sadness; breathe in prana, breathe out exhaustion; breathe in trust, breathe out despair; breathe in hope, breathe out anxiety; breathe in faith, breathe out insecurity; breathe in security, breathe out fear; breathe in energy, breathe out fatigue. If one breathes with this mental application, at the most basic level, it's good enough.

This is aware-halation. It will propel you towards your Shoonyam Quotient. Peace will come, as this slowly becomes a habit.

SPONTANEOUS BREATHING EXERCISE

Any time during the day become aware of your breath.

Watch the breath coming in.

Watch the breath going out.

Watch the breath retention, when it is retained in.

Watch the breath retention, when it is retained out.

Watch your emotional state.

Take in deep breaths, release gently.

Breathe in strength, breath out weakness.

Breathe in joy, breathe out sadness.

Breathe in prana, breathe out exhaustion.

Breathe in trust, breathe out despair.

Breathe in hope, breathe out anxiety.

Breathe in faith, breathe out insecurity.

Breathe in security, breathe out fear.

Breathe in energy, breathe out fatigue.

Take a deep breath, release it gently.

Practice aware-halation as many times in a day as you can. Expert help is recommended for breathing exercises in case you are an absolute beginner.

We also need to become aware of *how* we are breathing. Lie down and just start breathing, and then notice where you are breathing from—from your upper chest or your lower chest.

Next, to transform and transcend, utilize the breathing disciplines of deep breaths, conscious holding; deep exhalations, conscious suspending; taking your breath to various places in your body and strengthen a specific body part. Most people don't even know about cervical breathing, that is, breathing from the lowest ends of the diaphragm. The whole idea is to draw psychic energy from the navel, from your Mooladhara chakra because it activates your glandular functioning. For that, visualize breathing from the pit of the stomach.

Such breathing discipline improves the endurance levels and carbon dioxide tolerance levels. This empowers your heart muscles, increasing the quantity of blood pumped with each beat. This results in the sharpening and invigoration of your nervous system, transforming the autonomous as well as motor nervous system. This heightens your perceptions, as they are all connected to your breath. At the physical level, this also includes the digestive system and the time and quality of your sleep. You are regenerated and rejuvenated faster.

On the spiritual plane, watch your breath with no attachment, without being judgmental. When you are watching your breath, thoughts will interrupt you. Your attention will go to those thoughts. You just have to drive your attention back to your breath. Stay detached to those thoughts. Then, the gaps between the thoughts, the frequency between the thoughts and the breath, or both, will start diminishing, dwindling. Your breaths will get more and more refined; the attachment to your thoughts will start loosening gradually. You'll start slipping into the gap of consciousness gradually. And the aware-halation will be a vehicle for that.

Conscious breathing brings here–now. And there is bliss in the here–now because thought and mind can function only where there is distance. In the here–now there is no time and distance. In the future, there is time and distance. You can think about it. In the past there is time and distance, and you can think about it. In the here–now there is no stress because in reality there is no stress. There is only a situation and you deal with it.

It is such a wonderful thing that once you start breathing consciously in and out, breath itself starts to cleanse, to replenish, to reinstate and to reinforce. When everything comes together, your integration starts falling in place. By and by, your breathing evolves of its own accord. That's a beautiful sign—an unfolding, like that of the flower. From budding to flowering, and flowering to fragrance, there is no standard process; it is a process of being and becoming.

When you yawn, a little bit of drowsiness comes in. There is no thought, no plan to take a breath. It happens of its own accord. And that breathing out of the yawn is breathing out of sluggishness, and immediately we are recharged again. So a yawn could be an indication that your body wants to rest. Through the yawns, you are breathing out exhaustion and fatigue, because a yawn only follows a deep breath.

When your body needs food, you experience hunger, which is the body's way of telling you of its need. In any kind of activity in life, whether it's a focused physical activity or a normal physical activity, a certain amount of oxygen is needed to fulfil the demand of the muscles being used, to compensate for their wear and tear. Blood carries life force, nutrients, oxygen, etc. to the muscles. Muscles metabolize life force, oxygen and nutrients, and eliminate the harboured biological waste. That waste is put back into the blood for the elimination process. In this way, there is a constant exchange of energy at every level and metabolism takes place. A minimum amount of oxygen is consumed when we are sitting or standing, or even sleeping.

When your muscles are utilized, it's known as the breaking of your muscles or catabolic activity, and when they are being rebuilt, it's known as anabolic activity. Catabolic activity largely takes place in the daytime and most anabolic activity in the night-time, when the body is at rest. In some proportions, both the activities are constantly happening.

When walking or running, your body will want to breathe more to meet the increased demand. But if the body hasn't been disciplined, the activity will not last. Your muscle endurance, your tolerance and your stamina will not last. At times, you may have endurance in the muscles, but not have the stamina. At times, you may have the stamina, but your muscles will give way and this will lead to spasms. With breathing exercises, your stamina, your strength, your tolerance and everything else falls into balance.

At one point of time, the breath becomes so refined and so subtle that it is unnoticeable. In this refinement of breath, in the gaps, mutation of consciousness takes place. This shift to the mutation of thoughts, this is the Shoonyam Quotient. The glimpses of such a state could be very small initially, but gradually it grows and grows. And each stage of unfolding is unique. Furthermore, it is also unique for each individual. So there is no standard measure for it. This Shoonyam Quotient is your most natural state and it awaits you.

Get regularized, get Mickeymized!

Experience, Experiencer and Experiencing

9

It is said that human beings are creatures of habit. Once a habit is formed, it is very difficult to break it. One tends to get into the perpetuation of the habit because it creates a certain known path to walk down. A known path, just by virtue of being known, is comfortable and so there is a natural inclination to choose it. Whether we talk of the supposed 'good' or the supposed 'bad' habits, the inherent nature remains the same. We walk a certain path, then we feel that we have seen the path already and so prefer to walk the same path again. Before habits, however, comes the experience of something. It will be more apt to say that we are creatures of experiences.

We are constantly experiencing the world through our senses of sight, sound, touch, taste and smell. Each of these experiences sparks a certain feeling of either pleasure or pain. Sometimes we notice the small pleasures and at other times we totally miss them. Moreover, we only notice the effect of the experience in the form of such a feeling and not the experience itself.

While on the road, you may notice a baby peeping out through the window of the next car. You forget all that you were worrying about and are filled with warm delight. (A lot of us would, of course, insist on getting back to whatever we were worrying about as soon as the baby is out of sight.) We may forget the face of the child, but the feeling lingers on. And we would be able to recall this experience months later as well.

Even when we fail to consciously notice the feelings caused by the experience, they keep getting registered in our memories. At some level, the experience and the feeling it generates ceases to have a separate existence for most of us. That is the reason why we are prone to forgetting. And we opt not to experience incidents that do not produce a noticeable emotional charge. While travelling, you may not remember everything that you passed on your way to office, but if you are specifically asked about a landmark, say an all-glass building, you will recall that it was there. For every bit of information that you recall and remember, there is a huge amount of information that will not be recalled but has become a part of your memory.

So it is with all experiences. It is actually only a very small part of what you experience that you know or notice, or recall as your experience. You are driving through a neighbourhood and there is a beautiful fragrance floating in the wonderful breeze blowing through; but it could be completely missed by you. You might not know that you have experienced it. But later, if someone asks you, you might still recall it. You may fail to notice a junior employee from another department on the same floor as your office, till he is transferred to your team one day. And then suddenly you remember seeing him in the lift an umpteen number of times. Again, you might not be able to vividly recollect even one thing from a family wedding just a few years ago, even though you attended all the ceremonies and had thoroughly enjoyed yourself.

In Indian languages, the word samskara covers the entire gamut of experience, habits and patterns. It has a wider connotation than experience just as a feeling. Let's see how we can gradually use the word 'experience' to bring it close to 'samskara'.

Each of the examples illustrated above shows the nature of experiences and experiencing. It occurs in different ways to the same experiencer. And, at some level, the experience begins to have an existence of its own, separate from the conscious mind of the experiencer. In fact, that is how most experiences accumulate in a person's life.

Each experience, along with the emotional cloud around it, becomes a samskara and stays with you. As seen earlier, what we call experience most of the time is actually the feeling or the emotion that it generates. And every experience does generate some emotional charge, however light it may be. In a lot of ways, what we remember is a function of the density of this emotional charge around any experience.

Every such experience further leads you to a desire. Desire either to perpetuate the experience, to experience it again and again, or to avoid it. You may not even be able to track where the desire came from every time because the roots may be hidden deeply in the samskara.

The desire, the craving, propels you to do something to fulfil it. With a slight variation, the experience again gets firmly rooted in your subconscious. From desire to action, from action to more experience—the cycle goes on. That is the story of experiences in a nutshell. Or as the Indian scriptures put it, the 'samskara–vasna–samsara' cycle.

And then there is the experience of spirituality. Most experiences are more material in nature as they arise due to our interaction with the material world; the experience of spirituality is different. It is subtle in nature, compared with the gross nature of all we saw earlier. It is free of material interaction, even if it is arising at the same time as we interact with the outside world. It is coincident with such interaction but not the same.

If we start becoming conscious of our experiences, we will start noticing them. When we become conscious of the nature of our experiences, we start observing them differently.

We would gradually start noticing that what we call an experience is actually the feeling it has generated in us. Thus, the first step is to start noticing each and every experience: when you touch paper, when you are travelling, when you are sitting, when you are standing, walking, listening to music, listening to the chirping of birds, shaking hands or hugging someone, start noticing the experience.

And then also start becoming conscious of all your spiritual experiences while you generate experiences in other ways. These experiences do not need to be spiritual according to someone else's definitions, only according to your own experience of them. Whether it is meeting someone who fills you with peace, reading a book, chanting a mantra, engaging in an elaborate religious ceremony or visiting a mountain, just start noticing the experiences. You will also see the subtlety of your spiritual experiences. There is no way that you can miss their non-material nature. It will be more and more evident to you that the essence of these experiences goes beyond the material interaction.

Gradually, one starts questioning what separates the spiritual experience from other routine experiences, and how one kind of experience brings peace to one and not to the other. It will slowly start emerging that in the moments of spiritual experiences there is complete submission. The experiencer has fully submerged himself or herself into the feeling/emotion and become one with it. The separate existences of the experience, experiencer and the act of experiencing have fused and become one whole complete entity. It is easy then to fathom that every experience can become a spiritual experience only if we immerse ourselves completely in it and become one with it. There comes a point in time when the quality of experiencing is transformed in such a profound, irreversible manner that every experience starts generating the same enthralling peace, the same vibrant joy and the same conclusive fulfilment.

If you have a strong desire, it is an indication that the time has come for it to be fulfilled. And it is actually good that those desires are getting fulfilled. Desire after desire, you seek more and more. It can go no other way. The desires go on until you actually start craving for them, until you start seeking the ultimate. There is no way you can escape from reaching that pure way of being, being in the Shoonyam. Again, it is no coincidence that you are reading about that pure way of being right now. It is an indication that you are ready to take a dip in that state.

Ved, pure energy, together with pure intelligence, is the pure potential field of manifestation. It is in this potential field of manifestation that the eternal dance of creation takes place. And it is no coincidence that it is so vibrant. If it were not, this whole universe would be un-dancing, rhythm-less, stagnated and mummified.

The gunas (or qualities) of light, motion and mass have created this world for us to experience completely and set us free in transcendence. Instead, we humans are entrapped and enslaved by it. The purpose of detachment is defeated by our minds and ego, which see all existence in a limited, isolated and separated perspective. Attachment comes in as the fear of mortality is cast over existence. Fear of death and clinging to virtues destroys the very essential nature of our being.

Both the consciousness of materialism and spirituality should be balanced. Consciousness of materialism is the gross aspect, and the consciousness of spirituality is the subtle aspect. When balanced, the growing consciousness of each element of our totality progresses. And this growing consciousness, at its peak, should unconditionally be surrendered to the sovereign unbounded consciousness with the absolute trust of an innocent and uncorrupted, childlike mind. The supreme nature will then decide the utility and the purpose of our existence in surrender.

In the balanced union, integration and togetherness of oneself happens through the attitude of oneness, through the attitude of wholesomeness. It is in this state that there is no perception of truth; it is truth just the way it is. It is the state of the witness himself becoming a process, by virtue of surrender without prejudice. As the river flows without choosing its own course, only in the balanced union, can one call oneself a servant of the eternal being.

However paradoxical it may seem to us, it is in this state that anything can be manifested by us. Any selfless thought with appropriate intention when introduced into our being and left alone will manifest itself into material reality and spring before us. When desires are left on the banks of time and left alone in the right season, they will spontaneously grow into beautiful flowers and majestic gardens, into mighty trees and enchanting forests. It should be done with unflinching trust and faith.

If you look at manifestation through the eyes of science, just an intention creates a particular cluster of photons and then it creates a particular sequence of an electromagnetic field. This electromagnetic field goes on to create frequency-coded chains of energy and information. This sends signals down your nervous system, which in turn will become neuropeptides and then come out, once again to re-form everything in a particular way as sounds, images and other sensory experiences. For such a process of intention to manifest seamlessly, one needs to prepare a ground for it. Shoonyam is that ground.

In your journey and quest to find the ultimate truth (i.e., yourself or your soul) manifestation will unfold before you and seek you when you just surrender to the flow, dissolving yourself in the ultimate state of your being, the state of Shoonyam.

It's in this state of being and becoming, not doing, that creation really happens, because it is in the being state where you are cooperating with life and the course of life. You are responding—not reacting. Just being and watching, that's when the best chemistry in your life happens. That's the time, that's the moment: your transformational vertex. In such absolute consciousness you are an alchemist. It is the full awareness; in that awareness and consciousness, you are total. You are integrated; you are not divided. In the pure state of being, you are total.

Get specialized, get Mickeymized!

Food vis-à-vis Nutrition

10

Ancient wisdom says—you are what you eat. Your being will be your becoming and your consumption will become your manifestation. Food is such a basic part of existence that our world actually revolves around it in more ways than we think it does. It is not a coincidence that all celebrations in every part of the world feature a big feast. And for the most part, the feast is the celebration itself. Courtships happen over candle-lit dinners and major business deals are struck over power breakfasts. From community life to partnerships to individual existence, food is so central and yet, its influence and effect is beyond what the eyes can see.

Ancient Indian scriptures divide foods into three types: the sattvic (the pure), the rajasic (the tasteful) and the tamasic (the impure). The English translations of the words only denote the general direction and not the extent of their meanings. The Bhagavadgita, chapter 17, reads:

'Ayuh satva balaarogyasukhpreetivivardhanah l
rasyaah   snigdhah   sthira   hridya   aaharah
      saatvikpriyah l 8 l

Katvamlalvanatyushna teekshnarukshavidahinah l
aahara rajsasyeshta dukhshokamaypradah l 9 l

Yatyamam gatrasam pooti paryushitam cha yat l
uchchhishtamapi   chamedhyam   bhojanam
      tamaspriyam l 10 l'

'Foods that increase longevity, intelligence, strength,
health, comfort and affection, and are juicy, smooth
and stable and naturally liked by the heart, are
agreeable to the system, such are the foods liked by
a sattvic person
(These are the sattvic foods)

Bitter, sour, salty and too hot and spicy, dry and
burning; and giving rise to sadness–grief or ill
health–disease, such are the foods liked by a rajas
person
(These are the rajasic foods)

Food that is half-cooked, without juice and foul
smelling, leftover and old and impure, such are the
foods liked by a tamasic person
(These are the tamasic foods)'

The Shoonyam Quotient can be applied to food as
well. While the underlying guiding philosophy remains

the same, it is both easy and difficult to be present to the Shoonyam Quotient of food, simply because food is the one aspect of our lives that we take for granted the most. We consume food, but are seldom mindful of what we eat and how. As soon as we become aware, we achieve the Shoonyam Quotient of food.

It is very simple. You don't have to do more of something, but actually have to drop a lot that you are doing while eating to achieve this state. And it actually begins much before the food is consumed, right from how the food has been cultivated and produced. It is not just to do with the hygienic aspects of cultivation and production that are obvious to us, but also the more important and hidden ones. The good news is that the world is waking up and looking into these aspects now. Whether a loving farmer or a greedy multinational has grown the food will make a difference to its nutritional value. And we are now developing the courage to look into this and other such questions.

Even if one doesn't feel prepared to go to that level, there is a certain awareness that one can operate with once the food is available. Look at the food and see if it's the food that is luring you or something that is humming. What on earth is 'luring food' and what in heaven is 'humming food', you may wonder. Visualize a bright and juicy orange that lies in one corner. Food that is humming with life is like that orange. You will be drawn to it once you are quiet from the inside.

And now visualize a smoking-hot pizza with a generous spread of cheese and your favourite toppings. Your internal dialogue of chaos, the commotion occurring in the world outside finds a fitting partner in the food and you are naturally tempted beyond your right senses towards it. And, if at all you do not want to have it, there is a struggle within yourself. The struggle, which is no different from those in so many other areas of your life, is manifested here again.

The first one hums to you and the second one lures you. The awareness exercised in choosing between these two is your journey. So it is the choice of what you eat.

The next aspect is 'when' you eat something. This is as important as 'what' you eat.

Then comes the time when food ceases to be something external and begins to be a part of your system. When it is inside your mouth? No! When you physically pick it up? No—it's actually a part of you right from the time you see the food. And so, a complete experience of eating is one where you first satiate yourself with the visual aspect of your food. You look at it for what it is—the colour, shape, size and all other visual aspects. Not really labelling or describing it, but observing and experiencing the sight of it fully. Then you satiate yourself with the other sensory aspects as well. You smell it. You feel its texture. And then, when you finally put it on your tongue, tasting it with the smallest of your taste buds, you are completely one with the food.

When there is this level of oneness with food, when there is a deep sense of compassion and gratitude in consuming it, along with the mindfulness, then does one call it food or does one need a word more encompassing than even nutrition? Doesn't the person consuming, the food consumed and the whole process of consumption fuse into one? Clearly, this is the Shoonyam Quotient of food.

The Paranoid Humanoid jumps to the question: do we have time for such elaborate meals where we would notice every small detail? Well, one can always start with a small portion of a meal, expand it to one meal a day . . . and then before even realizing it, every time something is consumed, it will be with the Shoonyam Quotient of nutrition.

The 'booze' culture, the 'chocolate' culture, the 'ice-cream' culture, the 'popcorn' culture, the 'fast food' culture, the 'processed food' culture etc. is the flip side of technology. This was at its peak in the West in the sixties. We wanted mechanical food and that, in turn, makes us mechanical. This influences your thinking and emotions. This robs a person of sensitivity, benevolence and compassion. Food cooked by a mother for her child is a million times more nutritious than takeaway food. Here we are talking of psychic nutrition; when a mother's psyche, her complete love, goes into her cooking. That energy of love is reflected in the manner in which she looks at the food and even in the way she cuts the vegetables.

Nutrition is the food that primarily has sattvic quality, and finally is a combination of sattva and rajas. In modern times, you cannot have completely raw food. Sattva is 100 per cent raw. So today it would be good to have a combination of meals that have 70–80 per cent fruits, juices, salads and nuts. Periodically, you can have days and weeks wherein you consume only the sattvic raw food. Then, with that, renewal takes place. Because time, mass, space, motion, matter, light, causation and effect all take you away, eat you, reduce you. So this nutrition along with sunshine, breathing and the rest put together renews you. This creates a balance. A combination of breaking down activity and building up activity creates a balance that can achieve the Shoonyam Quotient.

Finally, I cannot resist the temptation of quoting Kahlil Gibran from *The Prophet* (The lines are beckoning us and not luring us, mind you!)

> And when you crush an apple with your teeth, say
> to it in your heart
> "Your seeds shall live in my body,
> And the buds of your tomorrow shall blossom
> in my heart,
> And your fragrance shall be my breath,
> And together we shall rejoice through all the
> season."

Get naturalized, get Mickeymized!

God, Spirituality and Religion

11

'*Agar Ramzan mein hai Ram, aur Diwali mein hai Ali; to kyon chadhti hai dharma ke naam par insanon ki bali.*'

'If Ramzan has the name of Ram (revered by Hindus) in it, and Diwali has the name of Ali (revered by Muslims) in it; why are human beings killed in the name of religion?'

—Anonymous

At a certain level, one realizes that transformation is nothing but a realization of your God-self. Now if your God-self is the all-knowing self, present-everywhere self, exercising-power-over-everyone-possible self, then you might have attained a lot of other things but not a transformation. If your God-self is the ever-balanced, all-loving, ever-joyful self . . . you are already transformation.

This is a book on the transformation of the gross and transcendence of the subtle, because we are not a solid static state of mass as we seem to be. We are fluid and dynamic. From the time we are born until the time we die—from the womb to the tomb—we keep transforming every nano-moment, without perceiving it. We keep changing, at the speed of light—almost 3,00,000 kilometre/second—since we are basically beings of light. But since the speed is very high, we cannot perceive it.

As in the case of a fan moving at a very high speed, the separate blades are not visible. What is visible instead is a disc.

Imagine, if we cannot perceive four blades of a fan moving at a very high speed, how can we catch something moving at almost 3,00,000 km/s? In the same manner, the realization of our changing selves is missed due to the limitation of our senses, in their ability to perceive.

Like I said earlier, if your God-self is the ever-balanced, all-loving, ever-joyful self, you are already transformation. Notice, you are not *transformed*, you are *transformation*—the eternal self-generating process. The presence of God doesn't escape your consciousness because your consciousness *is* the God-self; so what is there to escape? It is the all-prevalent phenomenon, as consciousness has no plural. You are part of the same being. You are here, there and nowhere in particular.

It's a vibrant existence where the difference between existence and non-existence ceases. The common perception of dualities gives way to sublime eternity—something that pervades all of your senses is yet beyond all of those senses. For someone who hasn't tasted it, this sounds completely nonsensical. And it is nonsensical—beyond the senses. It takes great courage to grab at something nonsensical. Only the courageous are able to go beyond the matrix of intellect perpetuated by the illusion of the senses. Transformation is breaking free from this bondage, once and for all.

What can be said about God that hasn't been said before in one way or another? And yet, how can one not say anything at all about God when talking of transformation? And then, how can one contain oneself and stop once one starts writing about God?

Oh God, Good God, My God!

Did you feel that the opening of this chapter is unusual? Different from the way one would expect a chapter on God to begin? And that's where we actually miss God—when we try to contain the great mystery either in a quantity or a quality.

Frequently, when we can't accept the great Indefinable, we declare it all to be a big sham or an illogical crutch for weak minds. And, at other times, we try to confine God in names, qualities, descriptions and definitions, get others to agree with them one way or the other and then negate everything that doesn't fit those descriptions. What we see in life as accidental is our inability to understand the core cause. From 'This is not it' to 'this is all it is', we miss the only mystery worth living for.

When we watch television, there is actually nothing alive inside it. It is only the dance of electrons on the screen that creates the illusions we see. Anyone who

watches television for the first time may feel there are
real people inside. Having lived with a television for
so long, we would only smile at this naivety. But if
someone familiar with how a television works looks
for those people inside the box, we would certainly
pray to God to give him some sense.

The boxes of religion only reflect the Great
Mystery, and we tend to make our specific boxes the
be-all and end-all of God and spirituality. This is so far
off the mark. If there is one topic that requires some
true out-of-the-box thinking, it is this. If you get lost in
the mechanics of religion inside the box, the dynamics
of spirituality will not be available.

The Great Mystery is in everything and yet is never
contained in anything. A true person of God, a truly
spiritual soul, a genuinely religious person knows this
intuitively, and for perpetuity, so he or she can see
that mystery everywhere—revealed and un-revealed,
in the profound and in the profane, in the impressive
and in the ordinary, in the sublime and in the most
ridiculous.

When a man comes to a realization of God, he wants
to share the experience with the rest of humanity. What
else is left for him to do? He has achieved everything
that a man can in one lifetime. He can only share it
with others around him. Others around get a taste and
feel of what he has done. And they throng around him
to get the complete experience of getting to know God,
commune with him and be one with him. As Rumi
says, moths are drawn to light, so are people drawn to
the brightest light of The One.

> 'Look upon these lovers who have become distraught
> and like moths have died in union with the One
> Beloved. Look upon this ship of God's creatures
> and see how it is sunk in Love.'[*]

Similarly, people are drawn to religions in the name
of God. Over the years, people keep adding to the
original experience according to their interpretation.
And a religion gets formed with its pantheon of Gods
and demi-gods, dogmas and rituals.

A fine thread of spirituality runs through all
religious practices. If it were not for a pure stream
of spirituality, no religion would survive the test of
time. In fact, it is due to the purity of this spiritual
core that a lot of poisonous junk that is passed off in
the name of religion gets neutralized and overpowered.
Without a strong orientation to the sublime, to God
and spirituality, no religion can survive, even if what is
visible is only dogma.

It is said that if you have faith the size of a mustard
seed, you can move mountains. It is a minuscule yet
infinitely potent truth; the essence of any religion
that is being referred to. If, by cutting through all the
claptrap of rituals and man-made customs, one can
relate to that grain of truth, only then is one truly a
person of religion. Not any specific religion, though
they may be associated with one, but a person of

---

[*] Subrata Dasgupta, *Awakening: The Story of the Bengal
Renaissance*, (New Delhi, Random House India, 2011),
pp 38–39

every religion. They are graced with the strongest possible glimpse of the splendour of the awakened state. And only these people who form the core of an organized religion keep it alive. They are the oil in the lamp of any religion, and not those hierarchical orders that seem to perpetuate it. The very essence of religion is lost in division. It is paradoxical, as all great truths are, that what really keeps a religion alive is, at the fundamental level, the eye to see the same grace in all the religions or a complete lack of fundamentalism in any form.

It is no coincidence that a particular religion comes into existence and evolves. All religions emerge from a single source. Sometimes it is a spontaneous combustion of providence in one person and at other times, a slow revelation as in the formation of dew on a misty night. Depending on the individual and the collective consciousness of a time, even a single book continuously reveals itself at different levels.

Religions get founded, thrive and vanish in a matter of a few thousand years. At best, they evolve and survive, and if the founder of a religion were to come back to life and see the present state of the same, he or she would be in for a big surprise.

Can anyone be so stubborn as to still insist on equating any one religion as THE only way to God-realization? The essence of each religion is the realization of the Divine, realization that the Divine loves you infinitely and to have gratitude for all that has been received.

Can we ever be thankful enough in life? Each one of us can go on counting our blessings forever. And a fervent gratitude is the highest prayer that one can ever offer. From this highest prayer alone the future of God, religion and spirituality evolves.

Look at the world around you. There is so much you can feel grateful about. If you can go on counting inexhaustibly, then you are really blessed. If you can find few things and have to think hard to find more, you are still blessed. It's just that you need to be more mindful of it. And if you can't find anything at all to be thankful about, then you are truly, profoundly and perfectly blessed, but you have completely forgotten it.

Go over your life and repeat the same process of finding out all that you should be thankful for. Start doing appreciation exercises—appreciating flowers and trees, yourself and your parents, the sky and the infinity of the oceans, the sounds of the waves and the drizzle. Aim to connect more with nature. The more you connect, the more the five elements you are made up of find a balance in you. Because you are nothing but a recycling of the elements: earth, fire, water, ether and wind. Stimulate these five elements. When you connect with nature, they get stimulated inside you. Then, very gradually, the ego gets shed as well, and your Shoonyam Quotient starts growing.

APPRECIATION EXERCISE

Sit down in a comfortable position.

Close your eyes and calm yourself.

Observe your thoughts.

Go over your life and look for all that you are thankful for.

Be in appreciation of each of them, slowly, one by one.

When other thoughts come, ask them to wait, as you are busy appreciating right now.

Go around the world and look for all that you can appreciate in the world.

Be in the appreciation of each of them, slowly—one by one.

When other thoughts arise, ask them to wait, as you are busy appreciating right now.

Go inside yourself and look for all that you can appreciate.

Be in appreciation of the source of all this.

Be in pure appreciation. Be the appreciation. BE.

Appreciation takes care of the ever-desiring human nature as well. The more appreciation there is in life, the less room there is for desires. The fight is not with desires, because there is nothing wrong in having desires.

Don't desire to be desire-less. Your desires will themselves lead you to desire-lessness. Look at it this way: every desire takes you higher. With every desire, you come to understand that desire itself is meaningless.

Every desire takes you inwards—seeming, becoming more and more meaningless. When this happens, it's an indication that you have arrived. It may appear that you are moving away from the centre, whereas you are actually moving in towards it.

And once all your material desires are fulfilled, there is a surge of energy, which seeks a slightly higher level of satiation. Then your mind turns to art, poetry and music. Once that is satiated, then what? Your mind surges upwards and ego is left behind. Ego is on the borderline when the mind gravitates towards art, music and poetry.

Keep fulfilling desire after desire, layer after layer, for it will take you to a state where you know everything the material world has to give you. And now all that you seek is a more meaningful satiation, a worthiness that could emerge from aesthetics—art, poetry, music, anything that generates a sense of beauty and grace. Aesthetics can lead to fulfilment and spirituality. Aesthetics is nothing but appreciation, wherein you enter a state of unity consciousness. Then you are an appreciator, not putting value on the art, but becoming one with the creator, trying to appreciate the nuances of the expression of the creation.

Once desire crosses the threshold of poetry and music, you see the source of all this beauty. What is the source of this beauty and aesthetic? At this point, the ego is annihilated and the searchlight is focused inwards. Till the stage of art, the searchlight is outward. It is still a human looking at human sources; there is still separation.

It takes a highly evolved person in a state of poverty to realize that all the riches and materialism are meaningless. For a normal person, only experiencing materialism up to the hilt will make him or her conclude that it is meaningless. A wise person realizes the futility of wealth without even possessing it. For him or her, wealth and its trappings are all meaningless.

Maslow's famous hierarchy of needs says that self-actualization is the highest need. What is being discussed here is something beyond self-actualization. It is THE actualization, where there is no separation. Everything and anything is one. There is no separate I from you, and all is one. For religion to be born within a person, he or she has to be fully satiated. Otherwise the religion (and all its prayers) will consist merely of asking and complaining, or enumerating grievances. Those are statements of frustrations, not of belief.

Kahlil Gibran beautifully writes:

'You pray in your distress and in your need; would that you might pray also in the fullness of your joy and in your days of abundance.

For what is prayer but the expansion of yourself into the living ether?

. . . And if you cannot but weep when your soul summons you to prayer, she should spur you again and yet again, though weeping, until you shall come laughing.

When you pray you rise to meet in the air those who are praying at that very hour, and whom save in prayer you may not meet.

. . . Therefore let your visit to that temple invisible be for naught but ecstasy and sweet communion.

I cannot teach you how to pray in words.

God listens not to your words save when He Himself utters them through your lips.'

Prayer is nothing but a communion of compassion, for the created with the creator. It is love—the sharing and exchange of love. It emanates from and acknowledges a point where the distinction between the creator and the created vanishes.

Religion can be a ladder or a slide. Approach your religion and all its practices with this awareness. Oneness will come with prayers and chanting. That is the first step. Going to the temple, lighting a lamp or an incense stick is the first step that can open the doors to spirituality to set you free.

When you shed the dogma and doctrines, rites and rituals, you are left with only the beauty and the grace. You go to the mountains, to the oceans, to the flowing rivers and the jungles and the forests to be one with the divine. Through this, you transcend organized religion.

Aesthetics both precedes and succeeds religion. When you reach the pinnacle of your spirituality, you start seeing the beauty inherent in everything. The world remains the same, but the seer has changed and that's how aesthetics will be the future of religion.

Art is unconscious religion and religion is conscious art. In religion, you consciously create. Art is not a conscious outpouring aware of spiritual powers; it is a natural flow. That is why Osho declared aesthetics and not ethics to be the future of religion.

Religion and spirituality are nothing but a journey from one level of aesthetics to another. Spirituality is the bridge that connects one beauty to another, from the objective to the unconditional, all-pervasive and omnipresent beauty.

Get revolutionized, get Mickeymized!

Sex vis-à-vis Worship

12

Devi asks:
O Shiva, what is your reality?
What is this wonder-filled universe?
What constitutes seed?
Who centres the universal wheel?
What is this life beyond form pervading forms?
How may we enter it fully,
above space and time,
names and descriptions?
Let my doubts be cleared!

Opening Sutra
Vigyan Bhairav Tantra

Meditation provides the first glimpse of the here–now and leads you to awareness. It is awareness that leads you to consciousness, which is abundant and vibrant. This chapter begins with the opening sutra of the *Vigyan Bhairav Tantra*, the book that is the source of all meditation. Devi, the consort of the eternal, primordial

Shiva, asks these questions just after their communion is complete and she is still rapt in its experience. Doubtlessly, the setting is not a coincidence. It is the perfect setting to start the conversation on meditation.

Meditation is the tasting of the here–now. For most people, the first taste of here–now, is in the experience of sex—the experience of forgetting everything else; just being in the existing moment, at the existing place. The world seems to stop spinning. Time seems to stop ticking. In a moment, the world ceases to exist. But most people stop just short of having a glimpse of it.

People get lost halfway even before they actually meet. They meet physically, in the flesh, but even before their pulse begins to pulsate together, before the atoms of their souls are exchanged and become one atomic fire, they are lost. Because of the mind, the ego still exists in some way.

The mind keeps individual agendas of sex alive, reflecting the agendas that one is so ardently pushing for in life as well. One is trying to prove, the other one is trying to push. One is trying to complete, the other one is trying to rush. One is trying to serve, the other one is trying to be served. Domination, manipulation, greed, cruelty, insecurity, anger—all these guiding emotions show up in bedrooms. This happens when the ego has not been banished. Where there is ego, absolute surrender is missing, the absolute surrender that will bring oneness out of two.

And then, what could be an opportunity to experience ecstasy or bliss ends up as an unfulfilling compulsion. What could serve as a ladder of elevation to another plane of existence ends up as a slippery slide taking you into a fathomless abyss.

But another situation is also possible. When sex goes beyond the physical plane, it gets into the quantum plane that is love. When it transcends the love plane, it becomes worship. When it transcends worship, it dissolves into non-being. Because then, there is nothing to worship outside. Everything is just one. Then, worship is a stage, not a condition. You are together with yourself and you realize yourself completely. That is the Shoonyam Quotient of this worship.

On the physical plane, you are always trying to connect to the point you came from. That is a fundamental craving. There are fish that swim all over the world in the vast oceans, but swim back against the current to that spot in the river where they were born. In a certain way, that is what is happening here as well.

As long as man is a physical being, he subconsciously and instinctively wants to connect to the point he comes from. He wants to rejoin the source.

Another aspect of sex is the pining of one for the other. Some try to fill what is lacking within them through acceptance by the other. But this pining could arise from fear or an opportunity to find a complement for fulfilment. If the stimulus is fear, its outcome is insatiable lust fuelling itself. At times, fear also manifests as aggression.

This does not mean that there is superiority in abstinence, any more than there is in lust. A man and a woman represent the two aspects of the way of nature, the Tao. Once you start looking at the

yin and the yang, the female and the male aspects of
the world, conflict will disappear. Conflict will give
way to confluence, domination will make way for
cooperation, selfishness will give way to generosity,
because you will realize that fulfilment will not happen
only through acquiring and fulfilling desires. If the
other person is left incomplete, the other half of reality
is left incomplete. How can there ever be fulfilment in
incompletion?

The Tao is both male and female, passive and
active, hot and cold, light and shadow. Many such
dichotomies emerge from human judgment, and
have nothing to do with the nature of cosmic reality.
In the yin–yang universe, neither is superior to the
other.

Lao Tse whispers to us through the *Tao Te Ching*:

Seen in the light of Tao,
Nothing is superior, nothing is inferior
When looked in the radiance of its own
Each thing glows in its own way
. . . All things have different uses.

Fine horses can travel a hundred miles a day,
But they cannot catch mice.

. . . All creatures have their own gifts.

Therefore, the one who desires to have right without
wrong,
Order sans disorder,

Is ignorant of the principles of heaven and earth.
. . . To refuse one is to refuse both.

From Chinese medicine that insists on balancing the yin and the yang, to the *swara* yogis who prescribe the balance of the *ida* and the *pingla naadis* (complementary breathing from the left and right nostrils), the underlying message is the same: until you balance the two parts, you cannot transcend. The imbalance of one leads to physical and psychological negativity every time. An imbalance of either element in the love life would also lead to similar negativity in the relationship.

In surrender, the balance is achieved on its own. In surrender, you are provided with what is the most appropriate for you at that point and doors open for you to connect at the spiritual level.

In the normal course of events, the connection stays on the physical plane only. On the mental plane, the connection takes place later. When the connection happens on the spiritual plane, one doesn't concern oneself with connecting at any physical point.

Sex is such a strong instinct. Everyone understands the force of it, but few care to use the strength that it can create. Fewer still realize the hidden power that can be used to channelize this energy to explore the domains of self-actualization.

Sex is such a strong instinct that you really don't have to learn anything. The overlap of the instinct to perpetuate one's species has been entwined with the sexual instinct. In fact, sex is just the channel of the instinct to procreate.

But, as with other instinctual practices in life, you have been limited to the mechanics and have forgotten the dynamics. Just as you forgot the dynamics of life breath—that you are supposed to breathe from the abdomen and not from the chest, with complete awareness—so also you forgot that two people are to meet from the depths of their emotional reservoir and not just at the surface of their passionate bodies. As with eating, where the natural instinct of involving the five senses has been forgotten, so has the complete surrender to all the senses in meeting oneself through another been lost.

Surrender to the moment. Give in to the moment. Shut your eyes and forget that you are a man or a woman. Start from becoming conscious of the other, then of the self, then just watch the separation and the fusion. Be aware of each sensation as it arises. And then let all the senses converge. Become aware of the togetherness, so you can sublimate into that oneness. See where there is the separation and that particular separation will disappear. It will dissolve. Let the boundaries blur. Come to the point of unity in consciousness, become aware of one moment, become aware of one place, become aware of one entity contained in togetherness . . . the universe being just an extension of it.

Once you experience what you experience with the above, you will touch the Shoonyam Quotient of worship (of course, you will also realize in a moment why it is called worship in the first place). When the positive and negative energies are completely harmonized within us, there is nothing to look for outside.

From one great mystery to another great mystery, you can keep moving. From sex to worship, from worship to meditation, from meditation to pure being and from pure being to pure non-being. So when are you creating this Shoonyam Quotient . . . Tonight? Today? Right now?

ONENESS EXERCISE

When with your partner, choose to make the experience an experience of ultimate oneness.

Surrender to the moment.

Shut your eyes and forget that you are a man or a woman.

Become conscious of the other.

Become conscious of yourself.

Watch the separation between the two. Where exactly is the separation?

Watch the fusion between the two. Where exactly is the meeting point?

Be aware of each sensation as it arises.

Let all the senses converge.

Become aware of the togetherness, become aware of the oneness.

Watch where separation is, and watch that particular separation disappear.

Experience the boundaries blurring.

Come to the point of unity consciousness: become aware of the moment.

Become aware of the place.

Become aware of the only entity—oneness.

Become aware of the universe being just this oneness.

Be in the oneness. BE the oneness.

Get spiritualized, get Mickeymized!

Reality and Illusion

13

However we presume that we think,
It is more that we are thought.

I've said before that in Indian scriptures, ved is light energy in its purest form. Another meaning of ved is pure knowledge or intelligence. It's not a coincidence because these scriptures talk of ignorance as the absence of light. In other languages too, English for instance, 'enlightenment' is derived from the word 'light'. Pure light energy and intelligence is the pure potential field of manifestation. There is no separation at the level of this field. It is the state of the pure un-manifest where anything and everything is possible and from which all of creation emerges.

The eternal dance of creation goes on to its own rhythm. It is as if the world is getting created and is getting destroyed every moment, every nanosecond. Without this dance, the whole universe would be un-dancing—rhythm-less, stagnated and mummified. The gunas (or qualities) of light, motion and mass have created this world for us to experience completely and set us free in transcendence. Instead, we humans are entrapped by it and enslaved to it. The purpose of detachment is defeated by our minds and our ego, which sees all existence with a limited, isolated and separated perspective. And attachment comes in as the fear of mortality is cast over it. Fear of death and clinging to virtues destroys the very essential nature of our being.

Our reality is space, the reality of space is emptiness, the reality of emptiness is infinity, the reality of infinity is wholeness, the reality of wholeness is oneness and the reality of this absolute oneness is Shoonyam, as it is perfectly in the centre of awareness.

Read the above sentence again. This time, one phrase at a time, and you will start absorbing what this sentence is trying to convey to you.

Whatever we may think, introspect or analyse, it is never complete. At best, it only feeds our prejudiced worldview, and a distorted sense of the world gets reinforced. In actuality, meaning arises from synthesis and not analysis, because wholeness is just not the sum of parts but more than that.

Look at your own life. You normally live out many personalities within yourself—those of a parent, a spouse, an in-law, a professional, a philanthropist, etc. These personalities compete within you to seek a fulfilment of their roles, eventually making a being that is at once complex, complicated and confused—the result being a hypocritical and falsified human.

One must not allude to oneself solely in terms of the various role connections, but rather be firmly rooted in one's own self, where the point of reference is not objective but subjective. And then the way you conduct yourself in any walk of life will be balanced and harmonious. Truth will not reveal itself by analysis or dissection; call it up, observe it selflessly and it will unfold itself.

It will be your pure way of being, out of which your conduct will flow. The compulsion to keep an assortment of masks ready for different sets of people and different situations will not be required.

All the seeds of mysteries are sown in darkness, when and where no one can take notice of them, but they unravel in the state of light—in the state of enlightenment. The reality here is that we are beings of light and light is nothing but radiance. That's the essence of existence. The whole universe is born out of light. That light is also a manifestation of consciousness that is unfelt, but can be experienced. It cannot be expressed, but can be experienced. It cannot be defined, but can be experienced. It cannot be quantified, but can only be experienced.

You have to be in that state and you can be in that state by stilling yourself. First come to the here–now, this moment. Realize that you are not the body, you are not the mind; you are the one who has the body and the mind. So who are you?

And the answer to an earnest question, as to an earnest prayer, is never far. You will arrive at the answer: I'm the quintessential spirit. I'm that soul; that bundle of consciousness, which is nothing but a togetherness of memories, desires and experiences.

Experiences, not just of this and the previous lifetimes, but those of the entire existence till date.

Your cosmic age is infinity; there is no beginning, no middle and no end. You can either go on and on, or you can be like the fragrance of a flower, which is left behind when a flower dissolves. We human beings are a seed of that flowering, that can dissolve into this whole cycle of being and becoming—what Buddhists call '*anatman*'. When you go beyond yourself, your identity and your ego, your notions of reality also collapse and a new reality emerges.

Reality emerges when it is realized that the eye-centric world is an illusion, an attempt by the part to negate the self. This part, the ego, is the true cause of all suffering.

Any point of view is determined by our perceived reality that stems from the state of our consciousness. When the totality of two seeming polarities comes together, they converge into wholeness. That is Shoonyam. It is that emptiness which is full of radiance and vibrancy.

When matter is compressed too much it dissolves and disappears. If matter has to be reduced to Shoonyam, one way is to dissolve it by compressing it. Alternately, in rarefaction or expansion, if matter attains the speed of light, it disintegrates and again dissolves. So, it can dissolve both ways. Some ancient Greek philosophers proclaimed that the world is nothing but air. Maybe they couldn't identify that air is nothing but the same energy in essence. The real world is nothing but empty space. Anything can be born out of it and all shall return to it.

Perhaps this is the Shoonyam Quotient. This universe is a journey from invisible to visible and back.

In condensation, air becomes vapour and then water. And in rarefaction, it becomes gas and ultimately disappears when it gets heated up.

The same principle of condensation and rarefaction applies to consciousness as well.

Everything stems from one source. Spirituality in all traditions has asserted this and now physicists are saying the same thing. Unified Field Theory says that everything in this world comes from one field. You can't tune into that one source by doing more things. For tuning into that source, you have to drop everything and grab the handle of stillness.

Stillness is like creating space. That space can then manifest everything. It works wonders. In space, you take a back seat and allow nature to function. You allow reality to manifest and realize itself. You should not interfere with the process of manifestation. In your non-interference is your being.

The very essence of being is cooperating and not reacting. Your response is in your being and this can allow you to encounter a compassionate response every moment of your life. And your compassionate response is non-judgmental. Within the non-judgment exists innocence, and in innocence there is knowledge, wisdom, and spontaneity. Because there is no memory, so there is no reacting out of memory. There is the innocence of the 'anaadi' (the one with no beginning) and the 'anant' (the one with no end), the innocence of the eternal.

The innocence of a child and the innocence of a wise man are different. The wise man has known everything; the child doesn't know anything. For the child, there is only one world and that is none other than oneself. There is no separation of the self from anything or anyone else. Psychologists have found out that the first trauma of a child is the discovery is that he or she is separate from their mother. From then on it is an endless continuum of separation from the world. And that is the loss of innocence in more ways than one.

You are you and I am I—this is the fundamental duality. With duality comes the ego. The more the child gets to know the world and its treacherous ways, the quicker the child loses the innocence. It is only in the Shoonyam that the child regains its innocence. For in that innocence is all knowledge, wisdom and spontaneity.

This innocence comes from being completely non-judgmental, being open and vulnerable, just allowing whatever happens to you to happen and not be defensive. Such a non-judgmental person allows life to be, will let another be what she wants to be and do what she wants to do. He does not obstruct anything because that is the flow. And in that moment, your slightest wish gets manifested.

Manifestation has three realities: the manifest, the sub-manifest and the un-manifest.

The manifest for the most part of our consciousness, we think, is the be-all and end-all of reality. All materialist philosophy, science and political–economic thought, which were the basis of the rise and growth of the western civilization, have occupied thought space to such an extent that reality automatically gets equated with this manifestation.

The un-manifest is where everything is just unchangeable. Just pure awareness and consciousness is present. From that arises—thoughts, desires, ideas and concepts—the sub-manifest state. And those, whenever given more space and intent, become the manifest on the material plane.

Un-manifest is the spiritual, sub-manifest is the quantum and manifest is the physical.

The world is born and destroyed at the same time so fast that we cannot keep pace with it. At the quantum level, atoms are created and disappear constantly. And all this happens so fast that it leads to the illusion that the world has a constant existence. This is the same as the illusion of a fan looking like a disc, when it moves very fast, instead of the three blades that actually make the apparatus. We, who take the blades to be a single disc, miss out on the reality of this on-and-off world.

And now hold this thought for a moment: at this very moment, you are dying and being born again. Imagine the infinite possibilities this opens up. Every moment is an opportunity for you to be whatever you want. Because it is an absolutely new existence, you have the potential to be anything and everything possible, even that which has always been in the domain of the impossible until now.

Only in the absence of a bright possibility, one that beckons you, do you end up embracing the same old patterns—of memories and old desires. Your transformation need not yawn before you as a long-winding and tedious process. It can happen right now, right here. It can happen with a quantum jump, without crossing time and space. Just embrace the right now, the right here, be in the now, the here, just be HERE–NOW!

Get to the level of the senses till you have gone beyond them. Sometimes it just might require you to use certain techniques within the realm of a particular sound, a particular picture and a particular pose, significant till you go beyond.

Did I say go to the level of senses? Yes, I did. Attributing significance to the senses sounds exactly opposite to the path of spirituality. But here, it leads to enhancing the awareness. Significance is a phenomenon in the domain of the material world. In the spiritual domain, where there is nothingness, there is no significance. So sound also is not significant. The visual is of insignificance. Touch, taste and anything that is sensed is insignificant. It is beyond sense and non-sense. The whole field of spirituality begins where sense ends because if it still makes sense, it remains in the domain of the mind.

Maybe, in the beginning, you have to start with the gross and then move to the subtle. The other path is just to drop the being and becoming.

At the primary level is being

At the secondary level is sinking in the being

At the tertiary level, dissolving in the being

For every area this becomes your Shoonyam Quotient. Do exercise—be in that, then sink in that exercise, then get lost in that, dissolve into it, so that the subject–object duality doesn't remain and that becomes the Shoonyam Quotient. Then try it with eating, then try it with sex . . . This is our formula for the Shoonyam Quotient. This is our vehicle for the Shoonyam Quotient. It's a no-formula formula.

Get self-realized, get Mickeymized!

Intelligence and Intellect

14

Of what use is knowledge that cannot be mastered;
of what use is the mastery that cannot be put at
your command?

Have you ever had an experience when your brain
seems to stop working, your intellect has given way to
a cloud of muddled thinking, and there is a frustrating
and hazy, all-pervasive feeling enveloping your mind?
You pine and crave for those times when you had a
sharply focused thought process, when every thought
appears clearly and crisply on the horizons of your
intellect.

So what's the difference between these two states?

People have often discussed the difference between
the brain and the mind. The physical organ brain and
the oft-debated, oft-doubted mind. For many of us, the
brain is the mind. But is the mind only confined to the
brain?

Consider an intelligence that is all-pervasive. Look
deeply and you will be able to see this intelligence.

Your lungs work as if they have a mind of their own. They keep taking in and giving out air, of their own volition. Your heart works in a similar way. And your kidneys. And all other parts of your body. And why just the larger organs, the smallest part of the body too act in the same way. A fingertip exhibits intelligence when you touch something hot—it moves away without you processing the information of the discomfort consciously.

A tiniest part of a holographic image shows the complete original image. Similarly, all of me is in every part of me, and every part of me is in all of me. The intellect finds it difficult to accept this. For the intellect, everything is separate and independent. It knows only analysis and can only find differences and differentiation. And so, the intellect is a perfect guide to fragmentation.

For a whole and complete existence, one has to give up the way shown by the intellect. One has to look at the existence as an integrated whole, in which every part is just the same existence in a smaller form.

In that unity, one can clearly see that intelligence is not confined to just one biological part, the brain. It is all-pervasive. And not just that, it is in tune with, and a part of, a universal, all-pervasive intelligence—an all-pervasive mind field.

I think of the mind as the software of the brain or the mind as the component of universal intelligence.

Is it possible for the finite mind to comprehend the infinite just by watching? Such a question emanates from this limited intellect. When you dream the next time, notice if you haven't already, that you are able to do, say and be those things that you never thought you could be if you were awake. If a dream is created merely inside your brain, how can it reach beyond the boundaries of your personality and identity? In some ways, dreams reflect the intelligence beyond what your brain can process.

We have developed almost a religion around the brain and the intellectual power that it represents. We have devised measurements to ascertain the be-all and the end-all of this world.

First there was the IQ, the intelligence quotient. As adults, we have to deal with many other quotients, such as EQ and SQ—spirituality quotient—which throw up dispiriting scores. As we keep growing, the equation keeps changing and a new dimension is added to the world of perception. (God forbid, if we were in the corporate world or a religious tabloid reader, there would be twenty more quotients to deal with and discover all that we were not good enough at!)

As if all those quotients were not enough, here comes one more—the Shoonyam Quotient!

No, the situation is not at all that grim. All these quotients are just approaches to provide pointers for directing our lives. They are not supposed to create more baggage. And even if they point to something missing, are they not really pointing to a great future that could be waiting, just round the corner?

Even if it were to be so, drop everything and take just one quotient. Why, drop even that one and get the 'zeroth' quotient. Shoonyam Quotient, the quotient of zeroness, the quotient of your spirituality and your being-ness. That quotient has all the other quotients contained in it. And if you have any other quotient at a high level, without your Shoonyam Quotient intact, the imbalance affects your life in more ways than you realize.

Unfortunately, the inhibiting quality of the brain, our intellect, confines us and we ignore our mind. Our minds are trained to be a bundle of conditioned reflexes, and also trapped in the bonds of limiting conditions. Our minds are pulled by the forces of polarities.

Start escaping the pattern and think out of the box; grab hold of new ideas. Go beyond the processing of the mind. This *is* a quantum leap. Stop thinking, be spontaneous, intuitive. Be mindful that all traditions involve stopping the processing of the brain. In technical terms, it would translate simply as the coherence of brain waves.

The brain doesn't like this because this is the only way it knows how to exist. The brain feels insecure if it doesn't function. It has not known any other way but to keep working. Recall the story of the genie whose only condition to his master was that he be kept occupied. Finally, when the master ran out of all that he could wish for and more, he put the genie to work: to dig a hole and fill it up, and continue doing the same thing till he was told to stop. He put the genie in a self-feeding loop.

That is how brains also work. Intellect is the manifestation of this restless genie that has not learnt how to relax, how to just be. It ends up creating Sisyphean loops for itself.

Portions of the brain carry information and energy from the cumulative lives lived but these can be tapped into only by stopping to think, in stillness, in the gap between thoughts, by slipping into this gap.

Mindfulness is striking the kind of friendship with this brain that it is able to be in an 'ever ready rest'—a mind that does not have to remind itself of its own existence, by constantly taxing itself. An intellect that can sit gracefully and not feel threatened if it is not called upon to do its duty.

There is a big and elaborate world that is created by the intellect. There are myriad myths built around how intellect is the most important aspect of being human. These myths keep perpetuating on themselves. The life of the intellect is very short and of that the productive, constructive life is even lesser. More than fuelling the vital life forces of spontaneity, exuberance and bliss, the intellect fuels the struggle and the effort.

There is fragmentation and isolation, a feeling of separation throughout our existence. There is isolation from the world. Our attention is always on the fragmentation, the past or future, never focused on the here–now.

Who needs to work constantly? One whose idea of the world is a place that is difficult to live in, and where things do not happen easily or of their own accord; a hostile world where things need to be subdued. And to do that, the ways of this world are to be understood, and used to manoeuvre it.

The world of Shoonyam is starkly different. In the world of Shoonyam, the ultimate outcome is assured.

Each component has its place and is aware of that place. There is perfect correlation. Intelligence of the highest order weaves everything to it, whether you are aware of this or not. Even though there seems to be chaos on the outside, at the fundamental and core level, there is perfect order. Each component has a wisdom from which it operates with ease and in harmony with all others. Each one seeks and gains unique manifestations, and unfolds for it. Synergies are perpetually creating themselves, not from a fear for survival but for the pure joy of creation. Existence is not coloured in the shades of survival but in the beautiful hues of vibrancy.

This is almost like the CST railway station, in Mumbai, on a normal day. There are thousands of people coming in and going out, alighting and boarding trains, the trains constantly coming in and going out of the station. There is hardly anyone, except for staff members or vendors, who stay at any specific point for more than a few minutes. For an outsider or a first-time visitor, all this activity would appear like chaos. But, if you were to go and ask the porter or the manager the reason for the chaos, she would call it a perfectly normal day, where everything was in perfect order. She accepts this as routine, the fact that every passenger is going to a specific place, has a clear destination, a clear procedure for the journey, with the routes clearly marked. Outside there seems to be chaos, but inside there is perfect order.

There are six trillion chemical reactions taking place in our body every second. Now imagine, if the brain were to record and observe every single one of them with intellect. The intellect would be completely bogged down because this would be simply beyond its capacity. It would be chaotic for the brain to bring order through the intellect. And yet, order is restored routinely, effortlessly, and without much song and dance. There is perfect order and everything is synergistically correlated. That is the power of the highest intelligence, which precedes the intellect you possess and feel so proud about now—individually and as a species.

As seen, this order and spontaneity is eternal and has been there even before your very first thought was formed in your biological brain. In that sense, it is the zeroth thought, coming from the original, all-pervasive intelligence. This zeroth intelligence is SHOONYAM. Tune into it and you will be beyond the mundane chaos that the intellect confronts. You will revel in the realm of bliss. Shoonyam is the state of all possibilities and all potential. Humans can exceed any expectation of performances. In the Shoonyam Quotient, the other quotients are not left out or isolated.

This zeroth intelligence is not a numbered entity. It is a field of the pure un-manifest preceding the first manifestation. And, in that sense, it is the mother of all manifest thought and reality. From there, you can jump to any reality, in any space–time, just in the fraction of a second, a quantum jump. And the only access to this zeroth intelligence is through dropping the millionth, the hundredth and even the single thought and becoming completely mindful: the mind being full of itself and nothing else.

EMPTY THE MIND

This is an open invitation. You can avail of it as soon as you want.

Get optimized, get Mickeymized!

Concentration vis-à-vis Meditation

15

'Empty the mind.
Mind the emptiness.
So watching the emptiness makes it full.'

—Tao Te Ching

Meditation is the simplest state of being. It is getting to be simple.

We find it so difficult to be simple. It appears to be the toughest thing to do, but there is nothing to it—just being. The only thing we know is doing.

We find it difficult to drop all the trappings that we think are absolutely vital for our existence: our sense of right and wrong, our concepts of good and bad, our preferences of appropriate and inappropriate, and our convictions of possible and impossible. And the most difficult to drop: our identity and our ego. We hide behind societal conventions and the compulsions brought about just by virtue of being a part of society. Any excuse is a good excuse to avoid being simple.

Hearing the word 'meditation' conjures up an image of a very holy sage, lost in something that is very tough, very mysterious. Basically, it's 'not-for-me' stuff. We try it sometimes, but give up most of the time and resolve never to try anything in the nature of meditation again.

In addition, there are so many techniques that we keep hearing about that confuse us. How many times have you found yourself asking in desperation, 'Can someone tell me just one technique of meditation that would work for me?' And you are not alone. Every seeker—and you are one, whether you like the word or not—deals with this question. The purpose of those techniques is not to confuse you. Their purpose is to make different routes available to you. Choose any of them and just start. Practice that technique as if that is the only one, play with it, have fun with it and decide if that is your technique.

And then you need to check: are you meditating or are you concentrating?

Meditation is the tasting of the here–now. Here–now in its time-less, space-less form. The here–now can be attained through thought-lessness and seeking a thought-less state. On the other hand, when you are concentrating, you are making a particular thought stronger and stronger. Any specific technique with its dogmas and set of elaborate instructions could end up leading to the fuelling of concentration.

Meditation leads you to awareness, which leads you to consciousness that is abundant and vibrant. The awareness of the here–now is at the base level. That actually is the beginning of the journey to the ultimate reality, a reality that cannot be described or even experienced, but one can just *be* that reality.

When I am meditating, I am aware. (Here the choice of 'I' is a conscious choice for you to participate in the experience.) This awareness gradually grows into consciousness—consciousness that I am conscious of; consciousness that the universe is conscious of. I am nothing but the universe and the universe is nothing but me. And there is only one I, which is the totality.

A glimpse into such totality has led people to exclaim 'aham brahmasmi' . . . 'analhak' . . . 'I am that (God)'. In a state of complete totality with existence, can anything else be expected? When everything is you, will not you be God? And this state is beyond even the world feeling like an extension of you. It is you and you are it.

So 'aham brahmasmi', is not a statement of arrogant power but a statement of oneness and the strength that arises out of it.

Concentration is focus on a point. Meditation is the awareness of the whole. It is *being* the point and simultaneously being aware of the whole. Concentration is not being the point—it is watching it, but being divided. Meditation is being the point, being aware of the whole and being one with that. Concentration excludes everything. Meditation includes everything. In exclusion, a draining takes place. The harder your focus and concentrate, the more energy you start losing. The subject–object duality persists because there is a subject who is watching and there is an object that is being watched, and there is no connection between them. In meditation, the subject–object duality diminishes and finally dissolves.

In meditation, the experiencer and the process of experiencing merge and become one. Division is transcended, and togetherness, harmony, synthesis and community are fostered. In the sense of inclusion, wholeness prevails and there is no drain on your energy; rather, it is conserved. It is in division that the energy is drained.

Insecurity is one of the invidious habits that we carry with ourselves constantly. In concentration, this insecurity shows up. Your mind starts buzzing with the thought, 'What will happen if I lose my concentration?' There is anxiety. There is greed; there is lust, ambition—both of which take you away from the process, not letting you enjoy it, not letting you do it well.

So whatever the meditation technique, you could end up concentrating, instead of meditating, and consequently getting all the above results.

When you are meditating and not concentrating, there is bliss and security because you are one with it, you are the whole of it. And if you are the whole, of all there is, what is there to lose? What is there to gain? Where is there room for any insecurity? There is no anxiety, no lust, no phobia . . . no ambition and no greed. You are deep into it, total in it. The manifestation is so thorough, so beautiful that what comes out of it is also beautiful. What emerges from it is beauty and grace.

If you really push too hard, you might end up getting something out of concentration, but it will never have any beauty and grace to it.

The very word meditation connotes that there is no standard procedure for it. There is no methodology. The moment you count from zero to 100 to relax your mind or go to sleep, it may not work because the very idea of sleep is to calm and lull the mind, but you are making the mind active by counting. Similarly, if there is any process or methodology that involves the mind, the mind will get stronger and you will never be able to meditate. The idea of meditation is to dissolve the mind.

The whole idea is to get to where there is no thought, to the gap between thoughts. Where there is a thought and the mind is involved, there is no point; there is no way you can get to the gap because you are constantly inundated by thought and involved in the process. Meditation is not doing a thing—it is being. The internalization of senses, the yogic practices of pratyahar and yoga nidra are also *doing* in a certain way. However, it is just a step to enhance awareness, refine your senses and come to a level where your senses are at the level of unity consciousness.

Visualize yourself holding a flower, appreciating the flower, appreciating first the colour, then the texture and then the fragrance of the flower. Appreciate the shape and then the complete look of it so slowly that sight, touch, smell—all the senses—are involved in it. You are now getting deeper inside the matter, even beyond the matter, finally coming to the source, exclaiming, 'Wow, what a creation!'

We have five senses to experience our lives. How do we merge them? By being still. Experiencing the experiencer is meditation.

When you arrive at the source, that is unity consciousness—your source and the source of the flower are one. The energy that is manifested in you becoming you—a human being—and the energy that made the flower a flower are one. That realization takes place only after the 'you' gets deep into the senses and you diminish. So in internalizing, you become so much more *aware* of your senses that you are no longer at the impact of the senses and, yet, you are rooted in what is beyond the sensory awareness. That is real awareness.

Doing so, you are reaching being.

Being is just dropping all your guards.

Being is action in inaction, cooperating with life.

When you start exercising, you may not be able to do it slowly or may not even be able to appreciate the merit in slow exercising. Sometimes, you will not have the strength to do it slowly, say lowering the legs while lying down. Slowly, the strength in your abdominal muscle develops and so also the awareness and realization of moving slowly. Finally, one day you are able to do it almost infinitely slowly, and you are able to hold yourself stationary in a posture.

As with the body, so too with the slowing down of the mind, the reaching of blissful stilling could also take a course of its own. Get static—get ecstatic.

Where there is a will there is a way. The will paves the way for itself. With meditation too, the way or the technique is the least important element. It is a will, but without obsession.

Allow discontinuity. Allow spaces in between for the manifestation to occur. Don't wait for the outcome of a thing, for then it will be very ugly. Sow a seed and forget about it. Let it grow on the banks of time. Then the beauty and grace comes to it. Because then Nature's will is also going into it.

Zen masters, who were carpenters, would go to the forests on being commanded by the kings to make a chair and they would ask the trees which one wanted to be a chair. They would inquire, and the question asked with deep compassion in utmost sincerity would receive a reply in the form of an indication.

A Zen master weighing fifty pounds could move a 1000-pound rock. All he would do is tell the rock, 'I love you very much, please cooperate.' Then he would wait for the right moment, which the rock would indicate, and the rock would become feather light. Then he would move it.

Everything has life and you can put life into everything. When you are connected from your core to its core, the connection is complete.

Even when a mother wants to save a child from danger, she is able to show such strength because she is connected totally to the child. It would not be physical strength alone but psychic strength. And you can do so without consciously thinking about it.

When you are not thinking, you can reach your best. You can show up as the best of the creation, beyond your own beliefs when you stop thinking.

Be intuitive. Be wide awake inside–outside. Turn the searchlight inward.

Modern physics is finally getting a glimpse of the power of the observer and the fact that the observer creates reality.

In the case of sub-atomic particles, it is the trail left behind that tells us of their existence. It is only when you are watching that they are visible. Attention is so important in life. If the attention is in the past or future, there is either anxiety or fear. No sooner do you put attention into consciousness than it lights up. You take attention away from consciousness and it dies.

Since you are manifesting every moment, why not surrender? In non-surrender you will undergo a lot of strain and stress. Where God wants to play, He will make you a tool. So, why not surrender and become a tool? When you become a tool, you are endowed with grace.

I remind you about all the techniques given in this book and all others also that you have come across: if you don't remember, then forget them. As soon as you remember any, just live it. Let no technique become a burden on your soul. No technique is worth the lightness of your soul. Any technique you use, live it, sing it, dance it.

Get potential-ized, get Mickeymized!

Sincerity

16

'Each one of us is as old as the entire biological kingdom. Our bloodstreams are tributaries of the great sea, of its total memory. The uterine odyssey of the growing foetus recapitulates the entire evolutionary past. Its central nervous system is a coded timescale, each nexus of neurons and each spinal level marking a symbolic station, a unit of neuronal time.'

—Edgar Rice Burroughs
Out of Time's Abyss (1935)

Human existence is represented in terms of time and space. And merely by virtue of that, human perception of reality is contained and confined by time and space. By achieving one's Shoonyam Quotient, one can get past this reality. To go beyond, however, one needs to be completely one with the zero state.

Instead, one spends a pendulum-like life, oscillating from one extreme to another, from one mania to another depression, from one addiction to another compulsion, from one lust to another craving. A number of times these polarities are so subtle that someone else might completely miss them. Like power-hungry religious sects or the 'holier than thou' philanthropist, they are just a swing of the pendulum and not a channel for liberation. From one bond to another bond, however glamorous and socially acceptable, the swing keeps one dazed, and blocks out a vision of the ultimate reality.

The great mystery of going beyond the swing of life, beyond the yo-yo of emotions, is revealed in numerous ways. Not once, but time and again. Oddly enough, we spend less time practicing what we believe in than justifying it to others. More than practicing even an iota of it, we enjoy fighting to prove that this is the right way, the best way, the only way.

We do everything else, but practice THE way we have come to believe in. This is the fundamental insincerity. The irony of ironies is that each way would ultimately reveal the same mystery. The Vedas say 'ekam sad—vipraha bahudha vadanti': the good truth is one; the ones who know say it in different ways. What is the point in proving that something is the best way? Use the way. Why go after wanting others to agree with your way and follow it? Go ahead instead, and follow the way yourself first.

And the ultimate mystery of mysteries revealed in all the books, revealed by all the teachers is realizing 'WHO AM I?' That's all there is to know. That is the only journey to make, the only path to traverse. It is in finding out 'Who am I?' that one sees reality distinct from illusion. The reality and the experience of it stand apart from the illusion and the experience of it.

In the illusion of the ego, one cannot think beyond the self and considers it the most important of all that exists in the universe. This emanates from the illusion that one's self is a spontaneously existing entity, separated from all other entities. When the veil of illusion is lifted, you can find the all-encompassing unity all around you. Every atom contains the universe in itself and every cell contains the DNA code of the human. Not only that, every human also contains the entire existence, its history and its future in the layers of his consciousness. That being true, one cannot stand separate from anything that exists. The realization of the real self moves through all the times and spaces of existence.

These times and spaces are manifested by each individual. German zoologist and anatomist Ernst Haeckel coined the phrase 'Ontogeny recapitulates phylogeny,' by which he meant that there is a direct link between individual development (ontogeny) and the evolution of the species (phylogeny). The most famous illustration of this link is human foetuses that develop gill slits because, at that early stage, they literally are tiny fish, emulating the order of the evolution of our water-breathing ancestors.

Dr Spock, in his classic bestseller *Baby & Child Care* writes:

Each child as he [sic. passim.] develops is retracing the whole history of mankind, physically and spiritually, step by step.

A baby starts off in the womb as a single tiny cell, just the way the first living thing appeared in the ocean.

Weeks later, as he lies in the amniotic fluid in the womb, he has gills like a fish.

This does not stay confined to the physical space. He goes on to draw this parallel further:

The child, in the years after six, gives up part of his dependence on his parents. He makes it his business to find out how to fit into the world outside his family. He takes seriously the rules of the game. He is probably reliving that stage of human history when our wild ancestors found it was better not to roam the forest in independent family groups but to form larger communities.

So much time—spanning millions of years—is repeated in cycles. Similarly, when we have a vivid memory we are transported to another place and another time, we literally recreate the time and the space of incidents far back in the past. Without much effort, present space–time gives way to that space–time, which our reasoning tells us existed in the distant past. But the reality of the experience makes all the separation disappear. Within a moment, you jump from one space–time to another. Is space real? Is time real? And the Creator of the alternate space–time . . . who is that?

Even though Einstein proved conclusively and empirically that matter and energy are not different, modern physics is still grappling with the reality of matter. It is difficult to give up the illusions one has. Illusion of matter: what it appears, it is not. What it is not, it appears to be. Even scientists find it difficult to give up this illusion of matter, when they have to accept that there is no matter at the sub-atomic levels . . . There is only energy, codified in a particular pattern. That is the reason this counter-intuitive nature of matter is read and taught in science classes all over the world, but actually appreciated by a much smaller group anywhere.

When it comes to your body, your mind and your spirit, the same holds true. Mere words do not encompass their true extent. A theory is best understood through living it and experiencing it. When you drop the illusions and go deep, you experience who you really are. And most of the process is carried out by elimination of the illusions that you carry; illusions that bind and restrict you. On the path of 'Neti, Neti' (this isn't it, this isn't it), you get to 'this is it!'

As enunciated by Parthasarthy, 'vairagya' is discrimination between illusion and reality, and disenchantment towards materialism. The path to self-discovery is paved with 'vivek', the power to discriminate, and 'vairagya' the quality of detachment. When there is disenchantment, either arising from or leading to, detachment, it is said to be an inner calling. The calling, the beckoning, is from the core of your being, and in the presence of this calling, you remain unaffected by the lures of the world. That is the moment of connecting with the source inside you.

Many have said the same thing before. This is my interpretation in the here–now. Buddha enjoined us not to become worshippers of the footprints left on the banks of time as being the only sincere thing you can do. Do not become worshippers of a Bible or a Koran or a Gita or an Avesta. Do not practice the tenets of any specific book, don't follow them or abide by them if you don't want to. But rather than fighting the fight for it outside, fight the war for it inside. Whatever your way, become it, live it, be it.

Get super-sized, get Mickeymized!

Cosmic Nutrition

17

The very word cosmos encompasses the entirety of existence. It is the manifestation of that one source, the void that we have been talking about throughout this book. All that you get out of its existence, out of it being there to nurture your being-ness, is cosmic nutrition. It could be from the planetary movement in the sky that influences your mind, as astrology and gemmology suggest, and it could be from the sunlight that nourishes your skin and your emotional health, with all other non-food nourishment in between.

It is easy to ignore non-food nourishment. We are so obsessed with food that it takes a different level of awareness for us to realize the importance of the aspects of food other than its quantity. Gradually, we start paying attention to the quality of food and to balancing the different constituents in food. That is when we become nutrition-oriented for the first time, in the real sense of the word. And then, there is the next level of awareness, being aware that only nutrition from food is not enough.

Other than the channel in our body that absorbs the food-nutrition, we also have channels that receive directly from the cosmos. With the senses of touch, taste, smell, sight and hearing, and through a feeling heart, we are constantly absorbing the elements that directly touch the core of our existence. When we attune ourselves to the grand forces and subtle powers of the cosmic grandeur, we nurture our souls through all these channels.

Get out into nature and be with the tides. Listen to them, watch them as they rise and fall. Feel the river flowing in all its magnificence, the breeze blowing in your face and see if you can smell the flow of that breeze—yes, the smell of the flow of the breeze. Do that with flowers as well. Absorb the fragrance of flowers, and see if you can perceive any other message from the flower through the smell or any other senses. The grass, earth, mud, herbs and all other scented existence; find something every time so that you can nourish yourself through them. Then try to go beyond and absorb something from all the senses; and then from your heart, the channel of love.

You can get cosmic nutrition from various sources—like visual stimulates—the colours you absorb, the grace and the beauty you see in the clouds, in the rainbow, in the horizon, in the setting sun, in the rising sun, in the full moon, on a moonless night, in the starlit sky and in total darkness.

Cosmic nutrition is for you to absorb through sound—the sound of the breeze, water dripping, water flowing, water trickling down streams, down brooks in waves, in a gale, in fountains or in raindrops. Primordial sounds, mantras and chants devised by human beings are the sounds that one may not be able to decode at a certain level of consciousness but the super conscious level of the soul decodes it, understands it and is nourished by it. Use those sounds as well. Intellectually, you may not be able to reason it out or comprehend it but at the soul level, it is received well only if it is listened to with deep compassion and without any reservations. When doubt creeps in, it erects a big wall that distorts comprehension and causes it to lose direction.

When you open your sensory channels and take in all that nature has to offer, which it does bountifully, you go beyond yourself and streamline the greater energies through you.

Cosmic nutrition is also a massage that releases and stimulates your energy meridians. Even rest is cosmic nutrition. Breathing and pranayam is also cosmic nutrition. In pranayam, you get connected with the totality. That 'awastha' (state) makes it possible for you to get connected to totality.

So anything other than food that nourishes you is your nutrition, something like a positive emotion, a compliment—'I love you', 'You mean a great deal to me', 'My life has changed because of you.' Or a positive reassuring closeness as when a child falls and the mother immediately picks her up, holds her wounded part and the child feels soothed, protected, secure—psychologically. That's also cosmic nutrition.

Whenever the condition of oneness emerges, and whatever triggers that oneness, it is cosmic nutrition. Whenever synthesis takes place, there is cosmic nutrition.

So it goes for all the senses. Whenever there is harmony and the melody is complete, it is cosmic nutrition. Then you can hear the universal music, smell the universal scent and catch a glimpse of the universal beyond!

One can't see bliss, but one can still experience it. That's when the Shoonyam Quotient of cosmic nutrition is achieved. Then you understand the meaning of existence, how it is meaningless and all that is meaningful is just consciousness. That is when you get connected to Shoonyam, the totality.

In the present time, the one big concern that surfaces when reading about cosmic nutrition is pollution. Pollution is a real concern, but like all other concerns, it shouldn't stop you from living and thriving. Consider that an inherent system in our body has a way of filtering pollution and combating germs, bacteria and toxins. If we give in to fear too much, we will not even be able to breathe. Then, it is better to get into the grave. You will be most secure there. To avoid death don't avoid life.

Environmental changes are inevitable. That is the way of evolution. If you breathe deeply and consciously, your system will likely get more charged up and geared to take care of that pollution. If people from the time when the concept of time as we know it today, say from the Harappan, Incan or the Mayan civilizations, were living in the present day with industrialization and its attendant poisonous chemicals, they wouldn't have survived in it. There would have been an instant plague and people would have died in droves. But, since then, our immune systems have adapted and they are conditioned to these pollutants now. Given the above, it is even conceivable that a nuclear holocaust might happen and some people may still live on.

Be aware of the pollution and contribute in whatever manner you feel is appropriate to deal with it. At the same time, have faith in the abilities of the cosmos, and the human body as a part of it, to thrive in the face of pollution. Because the human body is such an intelligent system, it is built to adapt to and combat all odds. As a compass always points towards north by default, so too, a human body, by default, always points to and tends to be directed to health, evolution, perpetuation, protection and the promotion of its own species.

For children to grow intelligently, they ought to grow on a diet that is a combination of natural food nutrition and cosmic nutrition. Natural food nutrition is an abundance of alkaline food, which could be raw vegetables, raw sprouts, whole grains, organic food, nuts, fruits, herbs, roots and seeds. Cosmic nutrition is available in the form of loads of sunshine, plenty of conscious breathing, abundant periods of rolling in the grass and loads of fresh air. Teach children the art of appreciating nature, looking at trees, the sky, the stars and the planets. Let them listen to the chirping of the birds and all sorts of primordial sounds—all of this nourishes them. Sight nourishes you, the tactile and olfactory stimuli nourish you, fragrances nourish you, a pat on the back nourishes you and a warm hug nourishes you.

Bringing up children with warmth and love paves the way for inculcating values in them, which enables them to see their place in the wider sense in this world. The greatest philosophical streams suggest that values are not just for subjugating the self, nor succumbing to societal pressure, but rather an important element for leading a balanced life.

'Ru Jia'—Confucianism's *Doctrine of the Mean* describes how one can create a healthy balanced state between the mind, the body and the spirit. By nurturing the mind, the health of the organs would follow. The guidelines for achieving this balance are to live with good manners, loyalty, honouring one's parents, proper conduct, benevolence and love.

Taoist guidelines for a healthy mind and body proclaim, 'Live with content'. Be free in yourself and be close to nature. Lao Tzu is regarded as the creator of the foundation of the Taoist philosophy. In *Tao Te Ching*, Lao Tzu stated 'people should return to the original condition of nature . . . complete personal tranquillity'.

Let nature take care of the healthy balanced state. Your participation should be confined to witnessing it, not interfering in it, not resisting or fighting with it. Watch it, be with it, observe it, cooperate with it and see things transforming around you. Whatever per cent of this you put into practice, you will see its manifestation proportionately. You will tend to interfere and not cooperate at some point of time, but then you will check yourself and things will just fall into place.

Get illumin-ized, get Mickeymized!

Being and Becoming

18

Life is a wonderful gift with which we are all endowed. We may not completely realize the extent of truth in this statement. We may even be deluded into believing otherwise. Life may actually feel like you are stuck in a rut or become a burden at times. But even then, it never ceases to be the gift that it really is. The truth and beauty of life lies in the small things that cannot be perceived by analysis.

Whatever happens in life has some significance. It happens because it is a part of your being and becoming. Even the least insignificant details of life: of actions, feelings and sensations that come with every movement of thought transform the moment. You start watching with deep compassion and you start cooperating with the cosmic being. You start witnessing with selfless devotional love, and you start becoming one with all that is, all that was and all that can ever be. In this state, your being is the field for becoming, with an appropriate response, for all transformation and self-evolution.

Apprehending this ultimate truth through analysis is difficult. Analysis creates confusion, more analysis leads to more confusion and then apprehending remains superficial, frivolous, a shallow collection of information. For real understanding, one has to know in completion.

If you understand only a part, your understanding is limited to that part. When you understand some of the parts, your understanding or knowledge increases, but it is still incomplete. Does it mean that knowing all the parts or all the facets makes you apprehend fully? Far from it! Do not hasten to feel joyous, as you are still limited in your knowing.

It's not just the part, not just some parts or even all the parts, but how all the parts relate and exist together as a whole. The very quality of wholeness, of completeness, of fullness, brings something that exists nowhere in the parts. It is difficult to believe at first. Once you start looking around, it will start to make sense. You will be able to see that the meaning of a sentence, the connotation, can never be fully known even if you know the meaning of each word.

The attempt to know wholeness is synthesis. Understanding emanates from putting parts together, and everything becomes more and more meaningful and in-depth as wholeness unfolds its truth in the state of being as it is.

Look at a sunrise. Look at the different parts that constitute the sunrise . . . the sun, the sky, the rays falling on the land . . . And also reflect on the different qualities of the sunrise, the movement, the spread of light and the increasing brightness. Feel each of the parts separately. Now feel the complete sunrise. Can you see the difference in analysis and synthesis? Can you get to the beauty that lies in the wholeness that synthesis leads to?

If you broke down a rose and separated each of the petals, do you think you could reconstitute it again? You can know the truth of a rose in all its beauty and grace. However, if you choose to gradually encompass each of the constituent parts with the awareness, it would dawn on you that the rose is much more than the sum of its petals.

Even in the ecological sense, Humanoids are tearing down the structures that have evolved over millennia by the powerful, seamless bonding provided by nature. Forests, minerals, atmospheric layers, all have been analysed and torn down. The process still continues. If a broken flower cannot be put together by us, what arrogance it is to assume that we can replace the ecosystems that we are destroying callously.

From external tearing down to the internal, the journey is just a complementary reflection. Even in thought, you cannot begin to see the tiniest glimpse of the truth as long as you are stuck in the analytical mode. The truth is far beyond the logical projection of analysis. But once you start looking at everything as an inherent and inseparable part of a bigger reality, it provides access to reaching the whole truth. There is humility in the process of synthesis, because the guiding thought is always incorporating the existence of something more, something larger and something that is beyond comprehension till now. And humility is the only vessel that can contain that grace, beyond the ken of imagination.

Truth will not open up to analysis or dissection. Truth will never be a slave to the intellect that wants to tear open the goose for the lure of the golden egg inside. Truth will not be subjected to revelation under rigorous autopsies.

However, truth is also gentle and yielding if approached through the heart. Call for it and observe it selflessly, and it unfolds itself. Confusion is always due to analysis—because your understanding is only that of the parts. In synthesis, you put the parts together and try to understand from the complete picture. As grace and beauty comes only to the whole, the sum total of parts is more than the total. Grace and beauty comes from the quality of wholeness.

This has a direct bearing on how we live. More importantly, knowing the true nature of analysis and synthesis creates a choice for us to live an existence that we really want to live. And every time there is a tendency to analyse anything, whether it is a situation or an event, life or the behaviour of a person, or even to analyse oneself, it would be a good reminder to stop and look at the ultimate outcome of this analysis, which is confusion.

Start to synthesize instead. Start to look at everything, to build up to the completion and totality.

From the thinking level, take the approach of synthesis to your living; and from living to your being. Isolated and divided, you disintegrate, you erode, you degenerate, and you become Humanoid. When you think that the way you breathe and the way you eat can be isolated from the way your business relationships and your personal relationships work, you are not looking at the synergistic synthesis that is the true interrelatedness of these. The inherent symbiotic nature of wholeness keeps adding meaning to it, ad infinitum.

When you attain ecological sensitivity, you expand your synthesis to be encompassed by the next level of consciousness. When you see the body–mind connection, how long can you not see the human–environment connection? Eco-sensitivity is not a fad to be followed or a just a bumper sticker; it is an essential milestone in the process of synthesis.

The existence of a human being stands for constant being and becoming. One is in the constant process of expanding consciousness. Each one is perfect in one's specific level of consciousness. Nothing is right and nothing is wrong. Everyone grows from one's perceptible reality.

It's in the state of being and becoming, not in the state of doing, that you are cooperating with life. The course of life is a flow as you are responding, not reacting. Just being and watching, that's when the best chemistry in your life is happening. That is the time . . . that is the moment . . . that is your transformational vertex!

When you try to grab one or more, you will succeed or fail in full or in parts. In the state of aware watchfulness, letting everything just be, you let the synthesis be. In that state of being, you are an alchemist and there is full awareness. In that awareness and consciousness, you are total. You are integrated; you're not divided. When you let everything be, you let totality be.

And how you do it is by first becoming calm and watching your breath. Just cut off from the rut. Come to the here–now. Sit quietly. Take a few conscious breaths. Breathe consciously in a very relaxed way. Being will happen. Transcending the subject–object duality through breathing, you will be able to transcend the subject–object duality through exercise as well.

A WAY TO BEINGNESS

Sit down comfortably and become calm.

Watch your breath.

Cut off from the rut of thoughts.

Attune yourself to the outside and cease all reactions to outside noises.

Calm yourself from the inside by silencing all the inside noises.

Come to here–now.

Take a few conscious breaths.

Breathe consciously in a very relaxed way.

Feel the beingness.

Transcend the subject–object duality through breathing.

Once ready, gently open the eyes to exercise.

Following the same process, transcend the subject–object duality through exercise as well.

The reality here is that we are the beings of light and light is nothing but radiance. That's the essence of the entire existence. The whole universe is born out of light to manifest itself.

You have to be in that state and you can do so by stilling yourself. First, come to the here–now, this moment.

You are, very evidently, not your name.

Realize that you are not your body. If you were your body, you would have been dead within a few moments of you being conceived, because ever since then, your body has been changing every moment. So much so that 90 per cent of your body's cells change in a year. Your body has been constantly changing and yet you are still the same for yourself.

You are not your mind. If you were your mind, you would have died the very moment you learnt something for the first time. Your mind changed that very moment. Through the changing thoughts every moment, you are changing your mind and, yet, your self remains the same.

If you are not your name, your body or your mind, who are you? You are the one who has the body and the mind. So who are you?

You are the quintessential spirit. You are the soul: that bundle of consciousness, which is nothing but a togetherness of memories, desires and experiences. Experiences, not just of this lifetime, or even the previous ones, but your entire existence till date. And your entire existence is the same as that of all existence that has been around. Your cosmic age is infinity, there is no point of beginning, there is no middle and there is no end to it. You can either go on and on and on or you can be like the fragrance of a flower. The flower dissolves and the fragrance is left. The process of flowering goes on. We human beings are a seed of that flowering that can dissolve into this whole cycle of being and becoming . . . this is what the Buddhists call the state of 'anatman'.

When we are not simple, we find it difficult to comprehend this state of being-ness. When we are simple, being reveals itself.

Being has three components: The first is the attitude—that of openness and non-judgement. Being open means neither positive nor negative about life—being non-judgemental about life, being non-aligned. The second component is the thought process. The thought should be of no thought. It should be thought-lessness. Pure here–now—attending to here–now, cooperating with here–now, and flowing in here–now. The third would be a behavioural pattern with no intent.

Being is more like being in the flow, cooperating with the flow. Moving with life and flowing with life—without a definite course. Being open, being vulnerable. Becoming is the outcome of it. Being with the flow means flowing with the stream of consciousness. Whatever the consciousness wants to do, whatever it wants to conduct, the way it wants to function on the material plane, on the manifest plane, your being is the cooperation with it. It is allowing the consciousness to blossom on the manifest plane.

Becoming is the realization of the being. As said earlier, being vulnerable, being non-judgemental, being non-aligned, and whatever comes out of it, is becoming.

Doing is going against the flow, ahead of the flow, beside the flow . . . Anything other than the quality, direction or pace of the flow. Basically interrupting, obstructing and disrupting the life force. That is why doing brings up all possible disharmonies. The smoothness is no longer there. The weather becomes stormy. Then there is frustration, obsession. We ourselves have to repress a lot of things out of lack of choice. All these become our negative shadows, an integral part of our personality and existence, and keep haunting us. And there is a collection of the psychological imbalances, emotional traumas, resentments, grudges, frustrations, obsessions, what we despise and detest, because this brings about a feeling of separation from wholeness. In the feeling of separation, the blame game and the victim–oppressor drama starts. The focus shifts outwards to find a suitable cause, a suitable entity to be made responsible for your situation, not looking inside to take the responsibility.

The first step of being is accepting the situation as it is, with deep love. Taking the responsibility for whatever is happening or has happened till date. And attending to it, co-operating with it—with deep love and without attachment to the outcome.

Becoming comes out of being. In a sense, becoming can also be perceived in doing. But if you want to look at the cycle of being and becoming, look at a seed. The seed doesn't do anything. It just is, just exists . . . and it becomes a flower automatically, when the time is ripe for the flower to manifest.

Don't take this to mean that being means tying your hands and not doing anything. It means attending to the call of the moment . . . and going with the flow. And then whatever actions arise out of it, just performing those. Which means, if you are hungry, eat! If you have to earn money, look for a job and do whatever it requires. Being only means no greedy chasing. You put your general, peaceful, non-aggressive efforts and let the efforts go free. Don't be attached to the outcome of it. Don't get obsessed, don't get frustrated if the efforts don't bear fruit immediately or if your desires don't get fulfilled at all. Because fulfilment is a process—time-less and space-less.

You may measure it in terms of a few days, months, decades, generations, centuries, millennia . . . but in reality it is its own process, and it has its own root and harmony to follow. So never get obsessed, frustrated or desperate. This will bring about destruction. Just go with the flow. If somebody asks for help, just help. Don't judge. Don't get into the whole 'the last time I helped him, he stood me up. She messed up on that. So this time I'll not help' mindset. You are obstructing the flow. The very fact that someone has reached out to you is reason enough for you to help.

Every time there is becoming, it is coming from your being even if you can't see that. Even if you feel it is coming from doing. Becoming is the becoming of life and it is karma at work. Here it is not just the becoming of your life. It is not even the being of your life. Being is collective . . . When you are participating with nature, you are in a collective mode. In the collective karma, we become a symphony in the harmony. We provide our note to the melody in the entire orchestration. So whatever it is, it is collective. And whatever it is, it will always suit the larger interest.

When you keep thinking whether it suited your interest or his interest or whatever he is thinking in isolation, it is not appropriate as it is a wheel. Becoming thus is said here in the special sense of outcome with your cooperation and input.

It is not that if you do not support, if you do not cooperate, life will stop. It will move on. It is a dynamic force. But if you are a part of it, you will also blossom and flower. Harmony will be a part of you. If you partake in the harmony of being, harmony will partake in your life. It will become a part of your existence.

To change anything outside, you have to change within. And all you have to change within is acceptance.

Flow and attend, cooperate. Attend with love, flow with love and cooperate with love. Become memory-less, become judgement-less, become opinion-less.

Even for something as inane as a movie, feel free to give an opinion, though that might also cease at a point of time. More importantly, when it is a situation affecting someone's life, don't partake in the direction of imbalance. When talking about the movie, bring totality inside. Be so total in whatever you are doing that there is no unfulfilled moment left to fulfil.

So there is no obsession, regret, repression, frustration carried forward . . . be so total in whatever you are doing, that the experience is wholesome and fulfilled, and each experience is the same, or rather it grows or becomes profound, either of the two or both. For somebody, it may grow; for somebody, it may be profound; for somebody, it may be multi-dimensional. As Osho says of peace: there is no way to peace, peace is the way. There is no specific way to being. Being is the way.

Anything that is drastic and life-altering becomes a breeze when you are in the being and becoming. It is smooth and blissful. Stress is completely out; there is nothing to worry about, nothing to be greedy about, nothing to lust for. You are so perfectly fulfilled in the moment of here–now that no other moment can fill up the gap. How would it? No other moment would have any space left for it. Because your consciousness expands, because your participation in the being becomes more profound, because every moment is good enough, the fulfilment grows.

And it can never stop. The profoundness can keep growing to an extent that dissolving takes place. Being and becoming is the taste of, a glimpse of, the eternal dissolve. It is a path to the eternal dissolve. You keep expanding and crossing limitation after limitation. Or you keep dissolving and eventually dissolve completely. So you reach, with either condensation or rarefaction, whatever you are talking about. You are either getting rooted deeper and deeper or you are going higher and higher, flowering more and more; or you are branching farther, and flowering more, with more fruits, more flowers, more colours. Or both are happening together. Everything is happening together and there is nothing to define. It is a process, which has no definite form. It's a process, which has no demarcation. It's a never-ending, eternal process. It wouldn't be eternal if it were any other way.

The first glimpse of being-ness a person can catch is in the morning when one has just woken up. One is awakened, yet the thoughts have not rushed in. These could be very few micromoments. But with awareness, these can be expanded and stretched. Catch these moments before the mind begins to chatter.

Be in these moments, cutting off from everything else. Get to the centre. Move out from the periphery. All this is not literal but very, very experiential. Cut off. Shut your eyes. In being and becoming, sinking happens. And dissolving happens. Sink into your being. Dissolve into your being and then meditate.

TOUCHING BEINGNESS

When you are ready to sleep, sit down comfortably.

Shut your eyes and take a few deep breaths.

Drop all the thoughts appearing in your mind.

With each breath, become more and more aware of the HERE–NOW.

When ready, open the eyes to read this.

Promise yourself that you will be waking up tomorrow with this.

Sleep peacefully.

When you wake up in the morning, wake up gently . . . with awareness.

Stay in the moments when the thoughts haven't rushed in the mind.

Stay in the centre.

Be in these moments.

Get to the centre.

Move out from the periphery.

Be in the zero state, the Shoonyam.

Be in the centre, experience it, and be in it.

Dissolve in it. Be it.

When the thoughts start rushing in, become aware of them rushing in.

Be grateful for those precious moments of tasting the being-ness.

Gently get up and get on with the regular activities.

Repeat the same in the night, extending the moments the next morning.

Get romanticized, get Mickeymized!

Death vis-à-vis Transmigration

19

'Under the wild and starry sky,
Dig the grave and let me lie.
Glad did I live and die and I laid me down a will,
These be the words on my grave for me:
Here he lies where he longed to be
Home is the sailor and the hunter home from the
hills.'

—Epitaph of Robert Louise Stevenson that
he wrote for himself

There are two ways in which we deal with the thought
of death. We either completely ignore it or we are
extremely fearful of it. Those who have never thought
of it find it irrelevant to even look in that direction.
There are very few who look at death in the right
perspective. Most look at death as the opposite of life.
Death is not the opposite of life; it's an integral part
of life.

As life is beautiful, so is death. What is death if not just another face of life? The fear of death, however, makes people apprehensive and takes them away from the beauty and grace of it.

Look at the sunrise, sunshine and sunset. These are nothing but the birth, growth and death of a day. The death of the day is the birth of the night, and so is the death of a night the birth of the day.

We are in the same cycle as the universe, being a part of the same universe and the elements of the same universe within us. If we are in the same cycle in the universe, why should we fear a cycle of living and dying? Life comes out of death and death comes out of life. They complement each other. Both can be lived to the fullest of joy.

How can you live death? By being completely comfortable about it! By not fearing and worrying about it, by not being anxious about it . . . by loving it! If you start loving death as much as life, then it will be as if life is the most blissful thing—for there will be nothing for you to fear.

If you love death as much as you love life then you will not fear anything. You will not fear impermanence because you will know that nothing is permanent. As sunshine comes and goes, as seasons come and go, as flowers bloom and die, only to dissolve in the earth and come back again as trees, and grass. The moon and stars in the night appear and disappear, so does our life. Why should it be any different?

Just because we think we can create the inertia of existence, we get attached to a state of existence and resist change in it. Just because our mind can create fear, just because there is so much attachment in Humanoid existence, we don't want to die. This resistance is only a reflection of lack of fulfilment in our life. We want to cling to something so that these temporary pleasures don't die. That is why in our temporary worlds we cling to everything that can give us pleasure. If you know right from the beginning that all this is going to go away, why would you ever fear it?

Death could be just passing away from your life, getting you into another dimension. Who knows which other dimension? Why bother, why fear, why ask? Did it matter which dimension you came from?

Being is life and becoming is the opposite of it. If you be in death, the becoming of it will probably be life. Let it just happen, let it just flow. Just live it and see what opens up for you.

Your life could culminate earlier by the factor of abuse. It could be brought about by the factor of fear and the factor of anxiety, by the factor of attachment or by the factor of erosion and disintegration . . . degeneration of self, your physical, physiological self, and your psychological self.

Alternatively, it could be that you are so fulfilled, you don't even think when death will have to come or when it will come or why it should come! It's just becomes a natural part of you.

Chuang Tsu once was in deep thought. When his students asked him the reason, he said he had dreamt the previous night that he was a butterfly. Unable to see what there was to think about it, as it was just a dream, they asked him why he was taken by it. Chuang Tsu answered that he was concerned if in reality he was a butterfly who was dreaming that it was a man.

Major philosophical schools of thought have discerned the fallacy of getting attached to visible reality. What is illusion and what is the reality is a question that bothers all of us. The ones who know have, time and again, shared the secret: it is all an illusion.

If everything is an illusion, let death also be one. In all of your perceived reality, if there is one thing that is certain, it is death. Even birth does not have that certainty that death does. There is no certainty that if there is intercourse, even if specifically to have a child, that birth will happen. But it is not so with death. Once the birth takes place, the death immediately becomes certain. The rest is not so. Life is so fluid that everything is possible. If death is so certain, why run away from it, fear it, ignore it?

Embrace it when it comes, when it happens. Not before time, but just in its time. In death, your real life force comes to the fore.

Death is nothing but the ultimate repose. It takes the life out of you and leaves you in a state of calm and bliss. That happens if there's no struggle for it. That happens if you've surrendered to life and eventually to that part of life which is known as death. It happens more so when you have embraced it as a choice.

Even surrender could be out of no choice. But embracing it is out of compassion. When there is deep compassion and love in your choice, you embrace everything and cooperate with life. You are not resisting it, because in resisting, you are going against the flow of nature.

Instead of saying 'why death?', we can choose to say 'why not death?' That incidentally, is also a statement: 'why not life?'

By not resisting either, we just flow in the river of acceptance. Just be, and you will become (what you need to become, the most at that moment).

A lot of people don't dread death as much as dying. Death is the continuity of a song when you pass away quietly, peacefully and with a smile on your face. Fulfilled and content with life. But the whole reality of your life is revealed in your dying. In your living, you can become the biggest hypocrite. But in those moments of dying, there is no space for the hypocrisy. The whole of your life passes in front of you in a jiffy. And in that jiffy, either there is fear or there is deep contentment.

Also, the energies in you being low (leaving for now they are not needed), all the things you have been suppressing all your life, all that you have chosen to ignore, will be overpowering. Dying is a process that comes about as the culmination of your life. It is a part of being and becoming. To choose your dying, you have to choose how you live. It's that simple.

Everything is energy and in death it transmigrates. It transcends form. What form will it take? You are the driver, you choose the direction. Make a choice. The choices you make now affect the way your energy transforms.

The world is getting born and getting destroyed at the same time so fast that we can't keep pace with it. This leads to the illusion that the world exists constantly. Discern the illusion from the reality of constantly dying and emerging creation.

From the time we are born, we are dying. Diseases eat you up. Entropy eats you up. The food that you consume consumes you in turn. The whole chase consumes you, and you are consumed in the Chase Maze.

Is the chase going to be your life? And is the chase ultimately going to be reflected in your migration to another state, another space–time? The chase erodes you. The chase disintegrates you.

From the moment you're born, you start dying. And from the moment you die, you can start living again. When you are dying, there's not a single atom in your body that you were born with. So who is dying anyway? And from this very moment, if you choose to be dying and getting born every moment, you can live every moment as a new life.

All the degenerative processes are inevitable as the process of life. But you can go past the impact of them. That can happen only when you have been enjoying everything with grace. The grace of being. Being in anything. You can be in sunshine, you can be in moonlight, you can be in *amaavas* (moonless night). You can BE in the flowers, you can BE in thorns. You can be in valleys, you can be in peaks. You can be blissful anywhere. Happiness and sadness are at the extremes. But bliss is in the centre. The centre where creation and destruction is happening simultaneously, where getting born and dying is happening simultaneously.

Imagine the infinite possibilities this opens up. Every moment is an opportunity for you to be whatever you want. Because it is an absolutely new existence: having the potential to be anything and every possible thing. Even that which has always been in the domain of the impossible till now. Only in the want of a bright possibility, one that beckons you, do you end up embracing the same old patterns, of memories and old desires.

From the centre, the Shoonyam, you can transmigrate to anything . . . any possibility, at the threshold of your imagination . . . and even beyond. That is the quantum leap that is possible this very moment, and every moment henceforth. Once you live your life practicing this transmigration every moment, there is never any death or dying for you . . . ever. There is only transmigration!

Get eternalized, get Mickeymized!

Bliss

20

Life exists in polarities. Everything and its opposite exist in the world. One can't choose to have happiness and expect sadness to not follow shortly afterwards. When either one of these is experienced, it gives birth to desiring. Desiring only what one feels and perceives to be conducive. But that's choosing only one half. By being present to both sides of the reality coin, one transcends the polarities. One transcends the desires. Desires disappear when the desirer is killed. And there exists a pure state of being . . . the state of pure bliss . . . that has no opposite.

You transcend desire when you see that the experience just IS, the experiencer just IS! There is only 'anubhav' and 'anubhuti' and nothing else. When you are able to see that there is an experiencer, you realize someone else is able to watch this experiencer. This someone watching the experiencer is the one who is the real you, which you never knew as any other than the one experiencing. The experiencer gives way to the one who is seeing, the one who is watching and the one who is a witness.

This witness is in bliss. Only this witness can experience bliss. And this witness can experience nothing but bliss. This bliss is not just a feeling, not just an emotion, not just an experience, though that is how we can conceive it till we reach it. This bliss is a state of being, where you are not experiencing it, you are actually being the bliss. You exist as that bliss, you manifest and radiate that bliss. When the experiencer doesn't collect experiences any more, he or she goes beyond karma, beyond the cycle of oscillating like a pendulum from one extreme to another.

This bliss is not only for some masters. It's for you and everyone else. Isn't that what every master also says?

The balance of Shoonyam is not a static equilibrium. It's not a dull or monotonous state. Dynamic equilibrium is the nearest that we can understand, though it is different even from that. It is a state of consciousness and consciousness is always fresh, always renewing. And 'dhyan' is your access to it.

Dhyan means mind beyond the self and the self beyond the mind. Dhyan keeps you calm, grateful; you stop hearing and you start listening to the eternal music with all your senses. One throbs with the pulse of the universe and flows gracefully like water. As water can break even a rock with its constant lashes and that is its hidden strength, so is the strength of your consciousness. Consciousness will prevail as truth prevails over everything.

In truth, the destructive patterns and emotions just stop appearing. Jealousy and envy are emotions, which are destructive, born out of possessiveness (greed and lust) and obsession (ego and repression). Have attachment only for detachment and detachment from attachment. Your actions will cease to be driven by anything but a deep love and compassion. Love that will draw bigger and bigger circles to take everyone in . . . circles so big that the concerns and botheration become invisible dots inside.

When every action will be an action with love, love will be in action. Transformation will take place as naturally as mud transforms into a flower, and a flower into fragrance. When transformation occurs, at times you fail to notice it. Why, you find it difficult even to visualize a transformed future. And that is again natural. As natural as the fragrance. Can you see the fragrance hidden in the mud? You also can't see the ceaseless spring of love inside you. You can't see yourself transcending the animal that you seem to be, the human that you think you are, to the divine that you really are.

Is that too grand for you? Do you think you deserve it? And if *you* don't, then who does? Even if you think you don't deserve it, can you still accept it as the divine gift? Does this scare you?

Give up all the fears. And choose faith instead. Fear and faith cannot coexist. As soon as you choose faith, fear will automatically disappear. Fear is nothing but faith in disguise, waiting only for you to recognize it.

In enlightenment, one accepts the truth of events in life with equanimity and repose. However, the enlightenment occurs only when one first operates with equanimity. Peace is the only way and there is no other way to peace. The wise one doesn't resist the turning of the wheel of change by getting impatient and agitated. They find solace in the hub, in the Shoonyam.

Look at the Shoonyam again. Right from the time of your birth right up to the time you breathe your last, you are never at a definite point. That is the reason limitations exist in your world. It is centring that brings you to the definite, stable point for the first time. Centring brings you to the domain of what is eternal.

You are centred, but not at a definite location. It is not in space, also because it is space-less and time-less. There is no location in space and no movement in time. In the 'sansara' you exist, as you exist in a wheel. Since the wheel is itself never stationary, your beginning and your end become arbitrary. The point of your start is not definite and the point of your end is not definite, because the wheel is always moving. It might start at this point and end at this point. Then, in the next life, start at this and end at another point, and so life goes on. Because of your desires and memories, you are constantly trapped in them. This is the chase. And you are trapped in the chase because you are not total, so it is generated by default. If you are consciously total, then all desires dissolve. Then the desirer is no more, and so no more are the desires.

You cannot do anything with desires like you cannot do anything with darkness. If you want to bring in light you have to switch it on. If you have to bring in darkness you have to switch the light off. Darkness is there by default. It's the light that is the reality. So whatever you have to do, it is to be done with reality. So to kill the desires, the desirer has to be killed. The desirer has to go. And the desirer can go only by switching on the light of consciousness.

The absence of being whole, being total, leads to the degeneration, disintegration and erosion of the being. It further feeds on itself and takes you into a negative spiral. That's the real insincerity. From being human beings, we become Humanoids—scheming, plotting and strategizing. We are so busy doing things that are constantly taking us from one level of un-fulfilment to another that there is no time or intention to enjoy the moments in life that bring fulfilment.

Anything and everything in existence is just perfect the way it is, as for all and sundry there is a role to fulfil, a purpose to realize in a location in space and a moment in time. Nothing is so big that it can't be learnt. Nothing so small that the details cannot be registered. For we can only master what we have known and command what we have mastered.

Being sincere is being true and experiencing bliss—which is beyond happiness and sadness—beyond the dualities of the materialistic world. This experience of bliss is the ultimate fulfilment of being one with the universal creative element, which in turn liberates every being.

Light and sound create radiance and vibrancy. The sound of light cannot be heard but felt and the light of sound cannot be seen but experienced. Let sound radiate and light vibrate. Let the light radiate and sound vibrate and resonate. One point of view is determined by our perceptible reality, which stems from the state of our consciousness. When the totality of the two (polarities) comes together, they converge into wholeness. Shoonyam is emptiness filled with radiance and vibrancy.

To go beyond the world, you have to go through it and not circumvent it. Shoonyam is the ultimate reality, right in the middle of the extreme polarities of the world. So be in the now and here to attain Shoonyam. The journey of Alpha and Omega is nothing but merely a journey from here to there in eternity, and finding yourself at a point, nothing different from where you started. As you started in now and you end in now, 'you are the light and the eyes that perceive it; you are the sound and the ears that hear it; and you are the wind and the wings that fly in it'. The proclamation 'aham brahmasmi' resonates from all of your being.

No sooner do you become total, conscious and aware—and all the three are one—do you see the whole picture in the largest perspective, where there is no beginning, middle or end but you still see it in the reference and context of here–now. And no sooner do you see it in the context of here–now that there is no depression or happiness or sadness. Because you know that the reference of the picture is here–now and everything is impermanent.

When you see that there is no permanence, that neither is your happiness going to last forever nor is your sadness going to last forever, you are in a state of bliss. In that moment of consciousness is here–now. That is why you are in bliss, in light.

That means when you are not total when you are eating something and thinking of something else, say sex, or doing something else at the same time, you are being something else . . . and becoming something else. You are a divided being, you have a divided existence. Your whole persona is disintegrated, you are getting eroded.

Humanoids are not just stagnating but eroding. They are disintegrating. Wholeness is putting those pieces together and bringing the light by getting those pieces together. When all the pieces are brought together, they complete the circuit and there is light. In light, everything is clear to you. In consciousness, you look at everything in the largest perspective, in the never-ending perspective, you are always in the here–now and you're always in the centre.

Because the centre always remains the centre, the here–now always remains the here–now. Time loses its perceptional value. Time depends only on where you look at it from. It is real only in a particular frame of reference. Even on such a small planet as ours, time changes every few kilometres.

Logic cannot explain and support the truth; it can be used for and against both ways. So it creates delusion. Confusion is the product of the schematic mind and clarity arises when one stops thinking and delves deep inside for integration.

We are trapped in illusions all around. Time is one such illusion. So is matter and so is space (distance).

What bring space into existence are objects. Space exists because you and I are there. If you and I were not there, it wouldn't be there and there would only be one infinite bundle of space stretched to infinity. The measurement, the finite, comes only when there is matter. The whole phenomenon of distance exists with matter, which is also impermanent and the measure is also impermanent. Illusions are created by time, matter, space, subject–object duality, light, motion, mass, and causation and effect. That is where dualities are created, black and white are created, good and bad are created and wholeness is divided, that is where the wholeness begins to erode, corrode and gets corrupted. Here–now gives you light, here–now gives you totality and in totality you are free. In totality you are free because in there is no fear and no greed.

How does totality give me freedom? Because when everything is infinite what do I fear and what do I yearn for? Why should I worry and what should I lust for? What is ambition and what is no ambition? What are scruples and what are no scruples? What is good and what is bad? Everything is just the same and everything is contained in that same seed. That seed, and not the constitution of it, is important.

As much as the flowering is important, so are the roots. But roots and flowering are not two different existences. They may look like they are. But in reality, they are one. Two hands look different in perception, but, in reality, they are one for they are parts of one body. Two wings look different but are one, being parts of the one bird. Taking it further, the wings, the bird, the flight and the wind in which the flight happens are one.

Shoonyam is lulling, lulling . . . refining your breath, refining your biorhythms . . . and coming to a level where there is complete coherence and you are in perfect harmony with yourself and without. That state of mind also affects your active state. The more you practice in meditation, the more it will reflect in your active state too. Eventually, you will be able to actively participate and be consciously instrumental in creating your reality.

At the being level, we are participating in the generation, operation and destruction of the whole creation/universe. As there is no single person who is God, God then becomes clear as an all-pervasive phenomenon, and we can see that we are a part of it. And in that sense, we become God by the spontaneous realization . . . I am that.

In dissolving, you become eternal; moment after moment eternity is experienced. Eventually, there is a chain of such moments, without interruptions, even if initially there are interruptions, obstacles and obstructions. Then the idea of death will be nothing but the idea of not being in this body any more. And the idea of life will be nothing but being in this body.

Dissolving in the being is the becoming of eternal consciousness, being the Shoonyam. Eventually, the being and becoming have to become one. There is no separation. The creator and the created merge together.

A time will come when Shoonyam will be a way of life for you. And you will become Tao, you

become Zen. You become Tantra. Nay, you shall
BE Tao, you shall BE Zen, you shall BE Tantra! You
shall BE the SHOONYAM.

It is difficult to understand the zeroth state because
it is uncountable.

It is important to take a dip in the Shoonyam state
because it affects the quality of the rest of the time, and
the activities and experiences during that time as well.

Shoonyam meals are supposed to nourish your
body.

Have you taken your Shoonyam dip today?

Get internalized, get Mickeymized!

Scan QR code to access the
Penguin Random House India website